This book is published strictly for historical purposes. The Naval and Military Press Ltd expressly bears no responsibility or liability of any type, to any first, second or third party, for any harm, injury or loss whatsoever.

Self Defense for Women:
COMBATO

CORPORAL "BILL" UNDERWOOD

(From the sketch by S. Schwartz)

Self Defense for Women: COMBATO

BY CORP. WILLIAM J. UNDERWOOD
2ND BATTALION (RESERVE), QUEEN'S OWN RIFLES OF CANADA

The Naval & Military Press Ltd

Published by

The Naval & Military Press Ltd
Unit 5 Riverside, Brambleside
Bellbrook Industrial Estate
Uckfield, East Sussex
TN22 1QQ England

Tel: +44 (0)1825 749494

www.naval-military-press.com
www.nmarchive.com

In reprinting in facsimile from the original, any imperfections are inevitably reproduced and the quality may fall short of modern type and cartographic standards.

CONTENTS

	PAGE
THE SCIENCE OF COMBATO	7
SAVE YOURSELF	11
GRIPS	15
PRACTICE AND APPLICATION	23

HOW TO MEET ATTACKS THAT ARE:

SIMPLE NUISANCES	24
SERIOUS BUT NOT DEADLY	34
DEADLY SERIOUS	78

Self Defense for Women:
COMBATO

THE SCIENCE OF COMBATO

"Combato" is an equalizer. It is a science designed to enable a relatively small person to meet a stronger assailant on equal if not better-than-equal terms by applying certain principles of balance and leverage and by attacking nerve centers where pressure or a blow will render his antagonist temporarily helpless—if necessary, permanently so. It is a science in which relaxation, awareness, and the element of surprise turn the attacker's greater weight and size against him. While it was originally developed as a technique for military hand-to-hand fighting, Combato is an ideal system of self-defense for women (as specially adapted in the following pages for their needs and physical limitations). All the original principles remain, as do most of the maneuvers, but there have been some omissions and several additions, since it is highly problematical that many women will be called upon to face a soldier with a bayoneted rifle and equally unlikely, we hope, that a soldier will find it necessary to deal quietly but firmly with a masher in the theater.

A great deal of mystery and awesomeness has always surrounded the Japanese art of "judo," or, more popularly, "jujitsu." It has been practically demonstrated that the Combato expert is the master of the Jap at what used to be his own game.

BALANCE In the Combato technique, balance is considered in two different ways. There is the sense of "being in balance," which means that the weight is distributed equally on both feet, the body is under control, and the hands and weight can be used with the greatest efficiency. The maneuvers that we will describe are so designed that while the assailant is kept off balance and his efficiency is greatly reduced, you, the victim, are always in balance and able to perform with the maximum efficiency, utilizing every bit of strength to the utmost. This type of balance is an absolute fundamental in nearly every athletic sport, from boxing to golf, and is especially important in the case of Combato.

Another way Combato students should think of balance is in the sense of "overbalance." Every one of us has a center of weight, or center of balance, and if we meet resistance below that center when our bodies are in motion, we tend to topple over. Witness "blocking" in American college football and the ordinary trip-up, and witness also Combato, for you will learn that you can meet force with force. Make your body block your opponent below his center of balance, and find that a judicious tug above his center of balance will lay him low. Your opponent's own weight is made to work for you and against him.

LEVERAGE In Combato, leverage is used to assist in overbalancing, to exert greater pressure on nerve centers, to make the various holds and arm locks effective, and, in general, to multiply the student's physical powers enormously.

If you have ever pried up a rock from your garden, or seen it done, remember what you did or saw and you have an example of the manner in which leverage can be employed in self-defense. A crowbar was pushed under the rock, a smaller rock or fulcrum was placed beneath the bar as near the base of operations as possible, and an amazingly light pull on the end of the bar moved an extremely heavy object. Think of your body as the fulcrum, the bar as an arm or leg of your opponent, the rock in question as his body, and the force used on the crowbar as the tug of your arms, and you have an example of the manner in which leverage is used as an aid in Combato maneuvers.

Of course the rigidity of the crowbar is an important factor in both operations; it already exists in the crowbar and is induced in the limb by locking a joint against itself. It is obvious, for instance, that the normal knee or elbow joint can be straightened just so far and no further.

It is to be noted in this connection that an arm, a leg, or a finger bent back on itself as far as possible has a minimum of strength left to make a recovery.

DIVERSION In studying the maneuvers we are to describe, it may occur to you to ask what your assailant is doing with his right arm when you have a grip on his left, since the arm is free and he appears to be in an excellent position to correct the inconvenience to which he is being subjected. The answer to your query involves another basic Combato principle—diversion.

You will find that in every case of this sort the grip you are shown applying is causing your attacker such intense pain that he has no thought for anything else. This fact, coupled with your speed of movement, plays a large part in many of the maneuvers.

NERVE CENTERS An attack on the nerve centers of an opponent can, if properly carried out, render him completely helpless. He is helpless in the sense that he is either paralyzed or is able to resist only at the expense of excruciating pain to himself. This form of attack is a component part of the many of the Combat maneuvers that you are to learn.

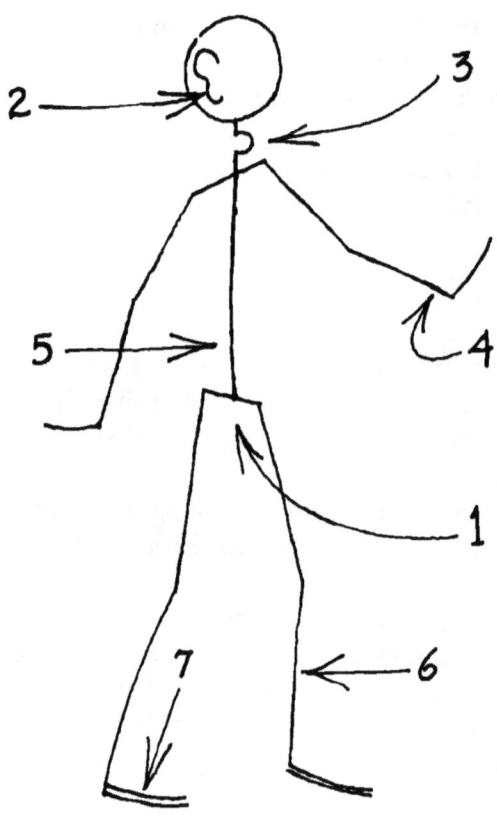

NERVE CENTERS TO BE ATTACKED IN THE COMBATO MANEUVERS
(1) Groin; (2) Head; (3) Adam's apple; (4) Wrist; (5) Kidney;
(6) Shin; (7) Instep

SAVE YOURSELF

One of the fundamentals in any physical endeavor is to learn to minimize injury to oneself. Combato is no exception. Among the first lessons to be learned in its study is the art of falling—which in our technique is a controlled maneuver that can be used to defensive advantage. The real secret is utter and complete relaxation of the muscles without losing control of them. The following illustrations will describe the methods to be followed, but it must be borne in mind always that the secret of success is *relaxation*.

To describe these falls in a system of self-defense may seem to be contradictory in a sense, for presumably, you should be mistress of the situation as a Combato student, but accidents will happen, and a lack of speed and co-ordination on your part may have permitted your attacker to steal a march on you. In any event, by learning to fall properly, you can save yourself injury in common, everyday mishaps.

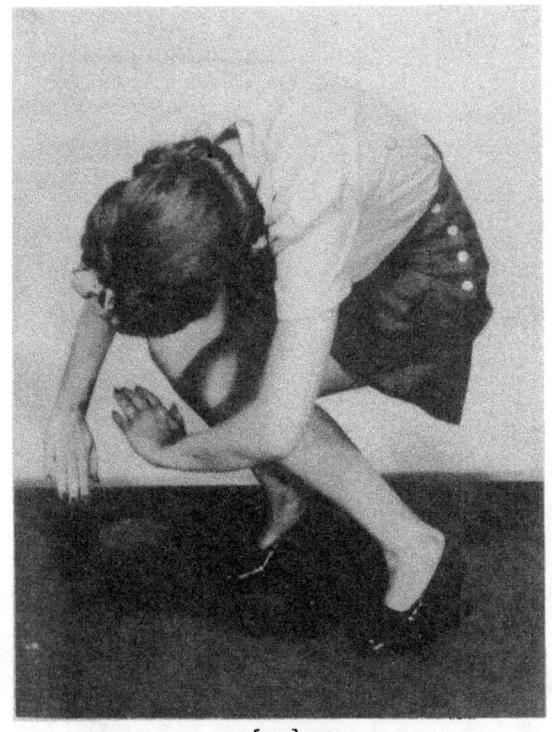

[1]

If you have been pushed from behind and it is inevitable that you are going down, roll as you fall. Protect your face with one arm (1) and break your fall with the other. Place your hands palms downward. Your shoulder will touch the ground immediately after your hands do and your head will be completely protected from injury. (2) Complete a roll and come up on your feet, face your attacker, and you are ready for him.

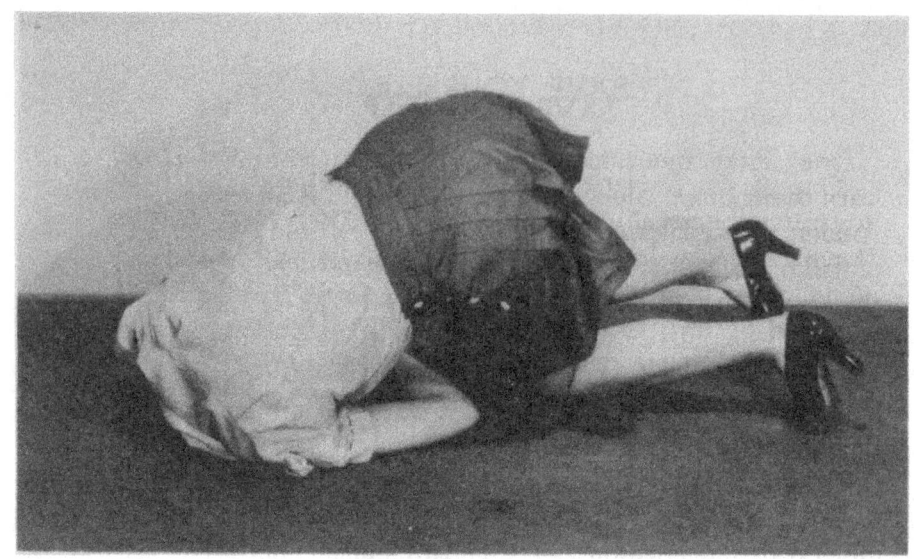

[2]

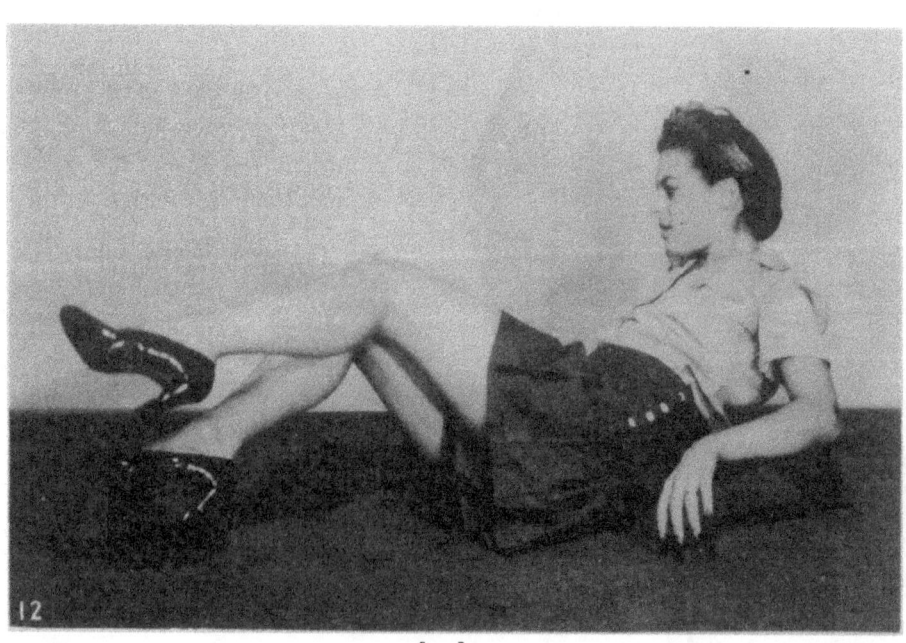

[3]

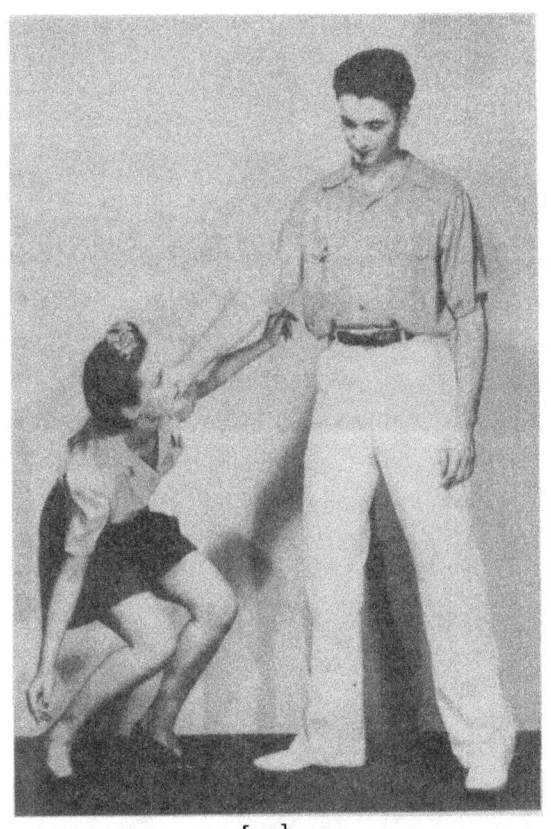

If you are being forced over backward, on the other hand, spread your arms, keeping your hands well away from your body with their palms down. Strike the ground as though you were treading water in swimming and simply collapse as shown, turning on your side as you do so. Keep your chin close to your chest to prevent your head from striking the ground.

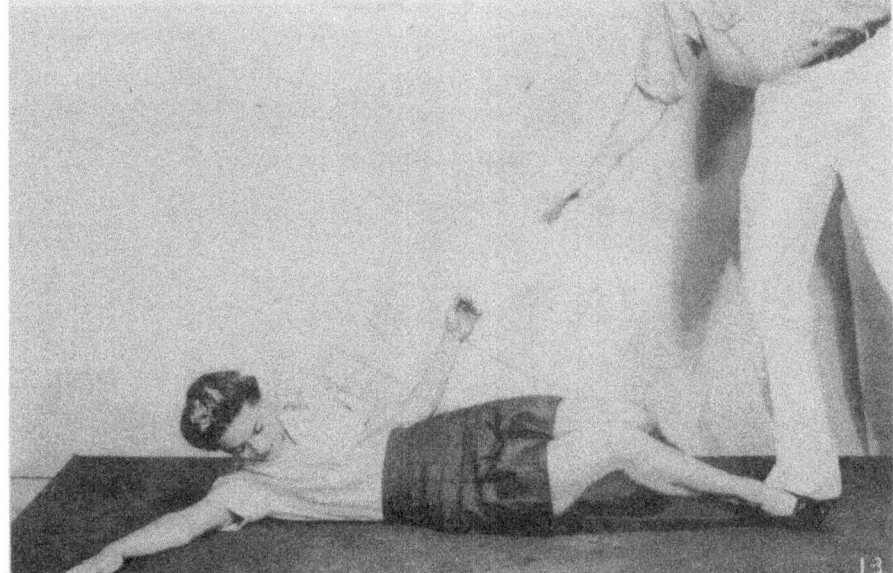

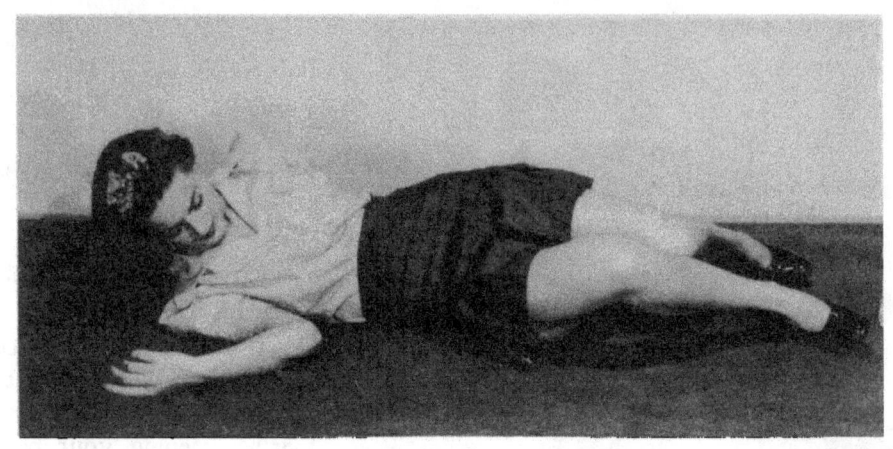

[3]

GRIPS

In order to practice any system of self-defense it is obvious that it is a fundamental to "come to grips" with one's opponent unless one elects to retreat (and retreat is possible). The important thing is to get the grip first and get it properly. The grips described in the following pages are devised in accordance with the principles of leverage and nerve pressure we have discussed; all are simple and practical, but all require speed and precision, which in turn means practice and loads of it.

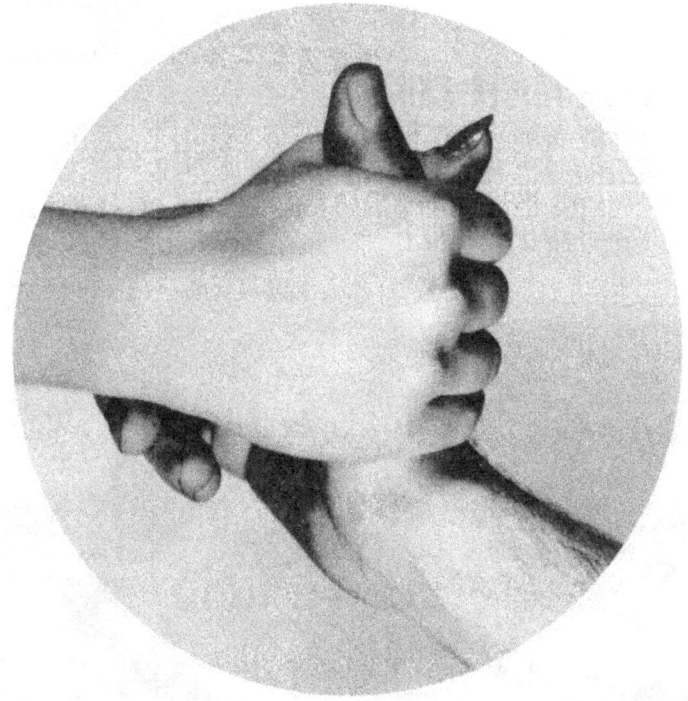

THUMB GRIP ※ 1

The illustration shows a simple thumb grip that is surprisingly effective for all its simplicity. Great leverage can be obtained with your little finger acting as the fulcrum, and your assailant can be caused considerable pain as his wrist is bent back.

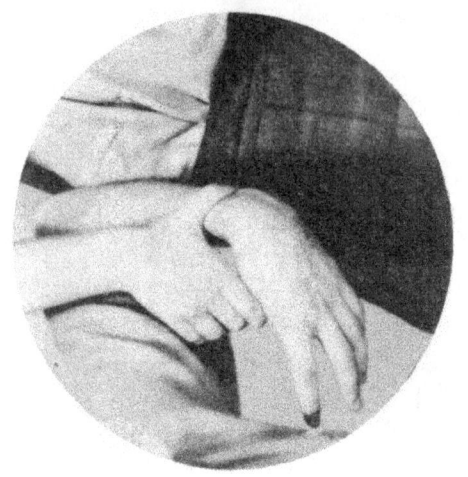

THUMB GRIP ※ 2

This might well be characterized as a "punishing" thumb grip, for it is all of that. In this grip, your assailant's thumb is grasped from *behind* his hand in contrast to Thumb Grip ※1. You pull his thumb back as shown and get your thumb on top of his wrist. Having done so, just squeeze, but don't squeeze too hard if you value your sparring partner.

LITTLE-FINGER GRIP

The little finger has relatively meager strength and it is vulnerable and easily hurt. This grip needs no further elaboration, since the illustration speaks for itself, but the results are astonishing when it is applied.

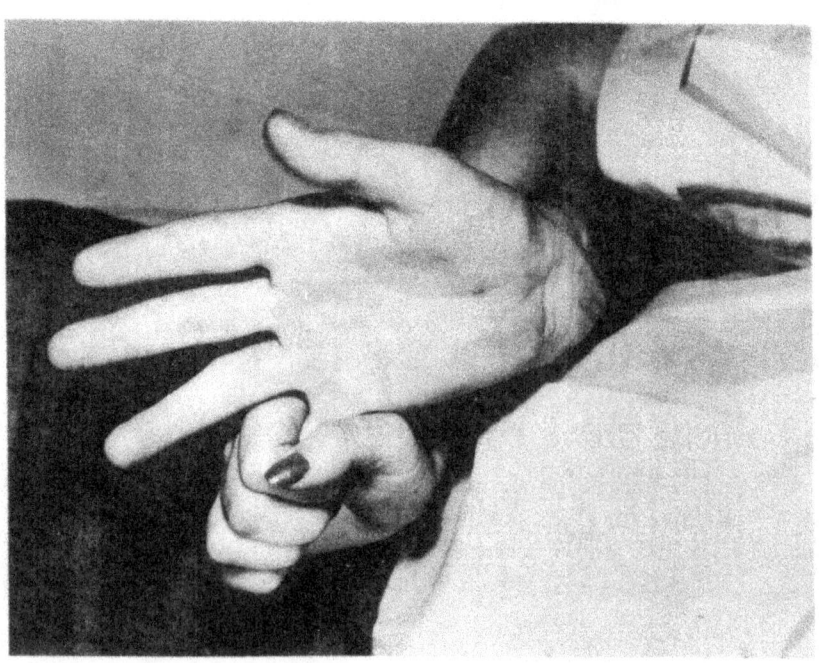

WRIST AND THUMB LOCK

The successful application of this grip requires the assistance of your other hand. However, the hand shown must perform the fast and sure portion of maneuvers to be described later, and its action is described here as a subject for practice.

Grasp your attacker around the wrist with the palm of your hand facing the underside of his arm. Slide your hand down and around until his thumb is imprisoned and your fingers are in a position to press against the nerve centers of his wrist. This seemingly simple grip will require speed and precision and loads of practice to attain them.

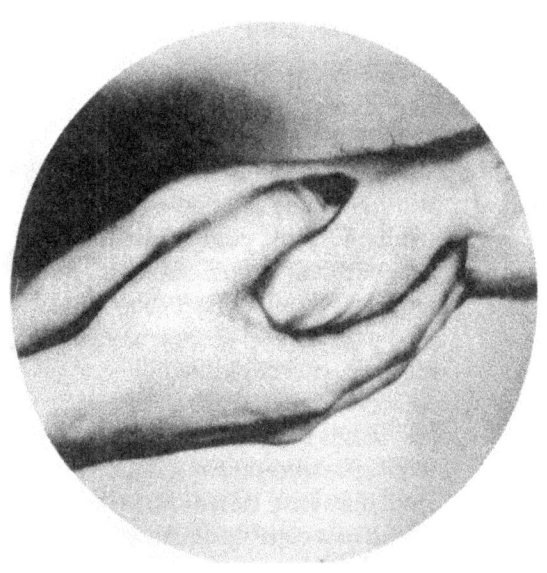

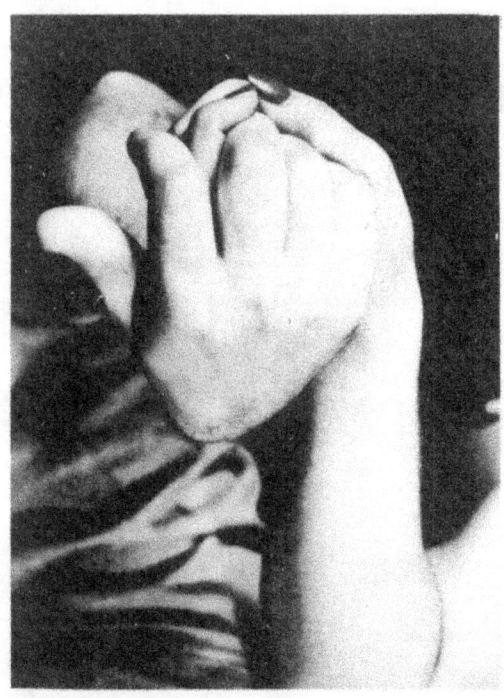

BACKHAND FINGER GRIPS

This is actually the preliminary step in securing one of the arm-lock grips. Two or three fingers of a groping hand are grasped from the inside and bent back as shown. The only trick to remember is to use the opposite hand to the one that is reaching for you. That is, meet right with left and left with right. It should be practiced both ways.

LEAD-OFF GRIP

This is a grip that is intended as a "persuader." It is designed as an effective means of leading away a prisoner and is as good as a handcuff. Slip your right arm through your assailant's left (A), grasp his hand over the top as shown, and then, pressing down on top of his arm with your left hand to provide the necessary resistance (B), bend his wrist down (C). This grip is capable of causing great pain.

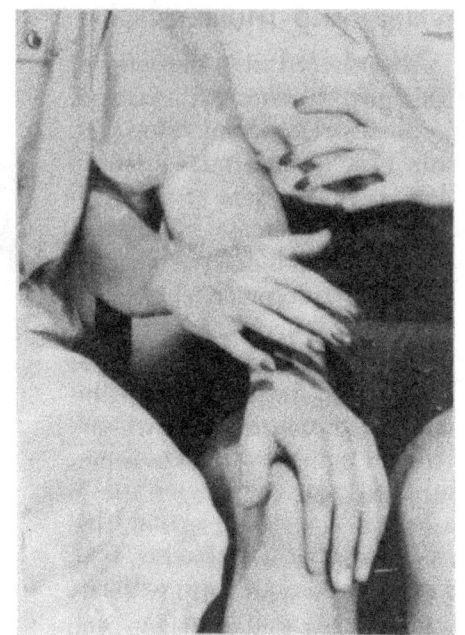

[A]

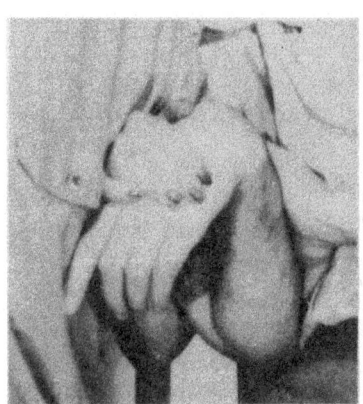

[B]

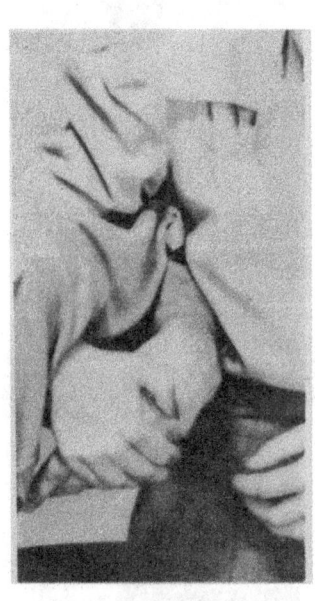

[C]

ARM GRIP

Here is one of the more complicated grips but one that is worth the practice. It was originally designed as a way of fending off an attacker who has grabbed you by the lapel of your coat or, in fact, any portion of your clothing that offers a grip. It applies equally to any reaching or grabbing attempt on your assailant's part that you are able to anticipate.

It is assumed that the attack is made with the attacker's right hand. Grip it with your left hand as shown in illustration (A), fingers around his wrist pressing on the nerve centers that are found there, and with your thumb against the back of his hand. Bend his hand inward, pressing it against your body, and at the same time take hold of his elbow with your right and pull it toward you and force his hand down so that it presses against your abdomen. His hand will be held tight against your body. Now shift your left hand and reinforce the elbow grip with it, as shown in illustration (B). By increasing the pull on his elbow you can cause him considerable pain.

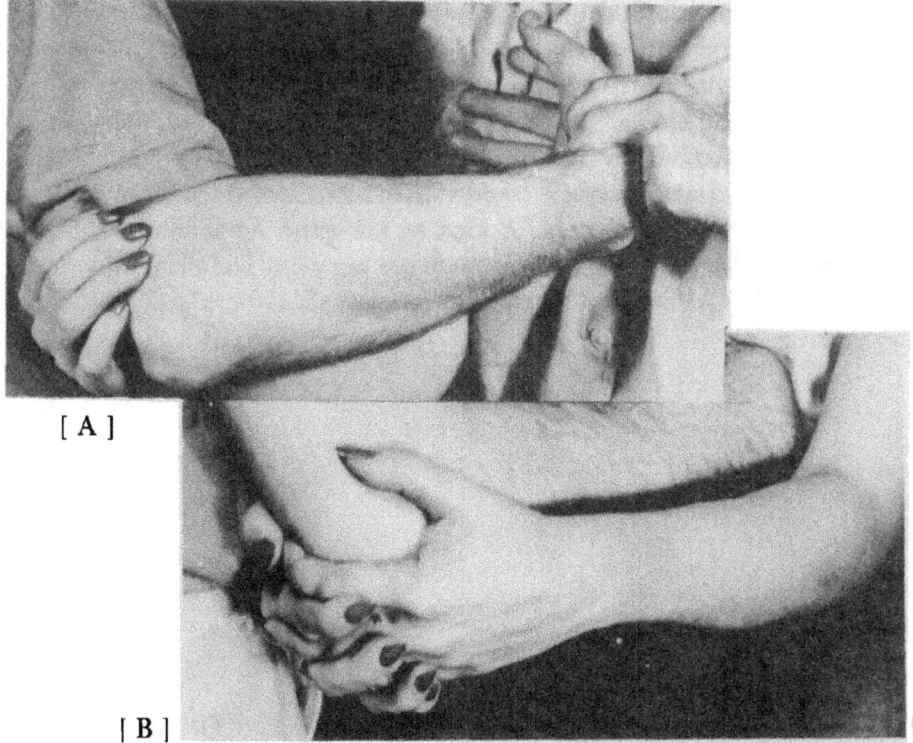

[A]

[B]

LAST STEPS

The reason for the diagrammatic sketches you will find in some of the maneuver sequences that are to follow is that it was obviously impossible to show the finish of the maneuver because of the danger of injury to the gentleman who portrays the villain in the illustrations.

In many sequences, too, you will perhaps wonder what you are supposed to do with your assailant when you have, let us say, a toe hold on him. Are you to sit there on his neck indefinitely or until help comes? The answer in this case is to let circumstances guide you. In all cases where this living-statue situation appears, the grip shown, if pressure is continued, can and will result in disabling injuries to the assailant's bones or muscles. If help is at hand and you do not wish to cause your assailant too much damage, simply hold him until you are relieved, but if you are alone and no help is in sight—fix him.

This slightly grisly but sound advice brings up the subject of "finishing blows." You will find reference to them throughout the text. They are actually disabling blows to nerve centers and are designed to render the assailant unconscious or temporarily paralyzed. A kick to the groin or behind the ear, or a blow on the Adam's apple are samples. The diagrams that follow will perhaps give you some ideas.

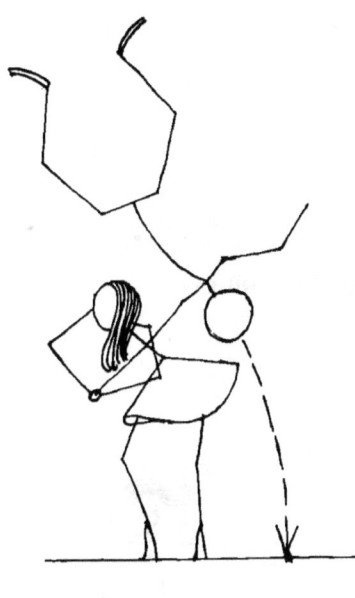

SHOULDER TOSS NO. 1

SHOULDER TOSS NO. 2

KICK TO THE GROIN

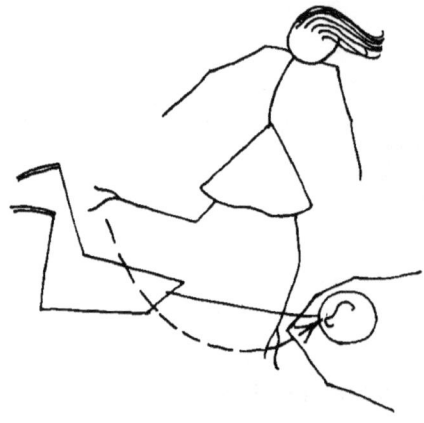

KICK BEHIND EAR

KICK TO ADAM'S APPLE

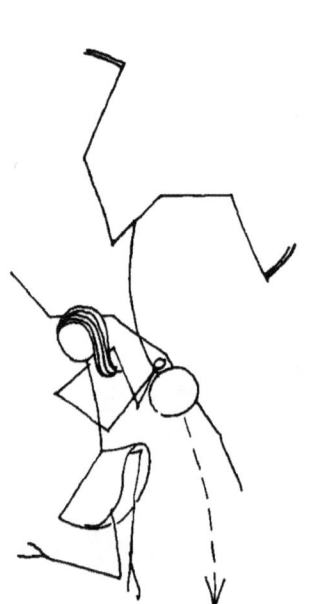

SHOULDER TOSS NO. 3

PRACTICE AND APPLICATION

Before going into the actual Combato maneuvers, let us sum up, in a general way, the elementary principles we have discussed. Remember first of all that our technique is a purely defensive one in which you take advantage of the momentum of the attack that is being made on you. Remember also that speed, co-ordination, and balance are of the utmost importance and that the science you are studying is, to a large extent, a mental one in which you must outthink, outgeneral, and surprise your adversary.

Combato requires no particular strength, but it does require timing. Timing, in turn, means practice and constant practice, and only by doing a thing over and over again can you so train your reflexes that you will act automatically and time your movements properly in a particular crisis. Begin by practicing the grips; do them over and over again for a definite period each day and do them in indiscriminate order; that is, don't do them ※1, ※2, ※3, and so forth, but vary the routine. Try them on friend husband or anyone who is convenient and good-natured; if necessary, stuff a glove. When you come to practice the detailed maneuvers, don't wear gym clothes; wear the clothes you wear every day. If you are accustomed to high heels, wear them as the girl in the illustrations does. The encounter you are equipping yourself to meet will happen without warning and there will be no time to go to a locker room. Relax, don't lose your temper, practice coolness and composure. Work out the maneuvers with a friend and try them often, but, when you are warned in the text, do not carry out the more dangerous ones to a final conclusion; it is possible that you might lose that friend.

The maneuvers we are to describe are designed to meet every type of violence the average woman is likely to face. In each maneuver the attack is arbitrarily shown as being made with either the right or the left hand. Realize that it may be made with the hand opposite to the one described and that your defense can be reversed to meet such a shift by substituting "right hand" for "left hand" and vice versa, throughout the description.

In a large category of violence it is obvious that there are degrees of seriousness in the mayhem that your assailant is attempting to commit. The man who is overardent scarcely deserves the broken collarbone or neck that the knife-brandisher has coming to him. For that reason, the maneuvers have been classed as "Simple Nuisances," "Serious but Not Deadly," and "Deadly Serious."

Let us first consider the

SIMPLE NUISANCES

The purpose of the "lead-out" maneuver is fairly obvious. It is a way of making someone go where you want him to, against his will. The illustrations that follow show three variations of it, designed as a means of coping with everyday annoyances. Realize, however, that these are serious grips—suitable for police work as well as for meeting the relatively minor emergencies that are shown.

MANEUVER 1

Among the minor inconveniences of life is an unwanted embrace from behind. It can easily be broken by grasping one of gay Lothario's little fingers. Give it a tug or twist and he'll let go. (See grip shown on page 16.)

MANEUVER 2

This sequence starts with an all-too-familiar gesture on the part of the gentleman who is seated next you in the theater. Simply apply grip, which is described in detail on page 18. It can be applied

[1]

[2]

with either of your hands, depending upon which side of you the attack originates. He can be quickly quelled, badly hurt from the pressure on his wrist, and, if you feel it necessary, escorted from the scene.

[4]

[3]

27

[1]

MANEUVER 3

This sequence is another of the "lead-outs" intended as a means of dealing with a character who won't go home when he should (1). He is seated with his left hand palm down. Reach over his arm and grasp it from below, as shown, with your left hand (2), and place your right hand un-

[2]

der his elbow. Turn his arm around and over, straightening it out with pressure on his elbow (3). You can force him to rise and create terrific leverage by forcing your right shoulder under his left armpit (4). This is a perfect exemple of applied leverage as described on page 8.

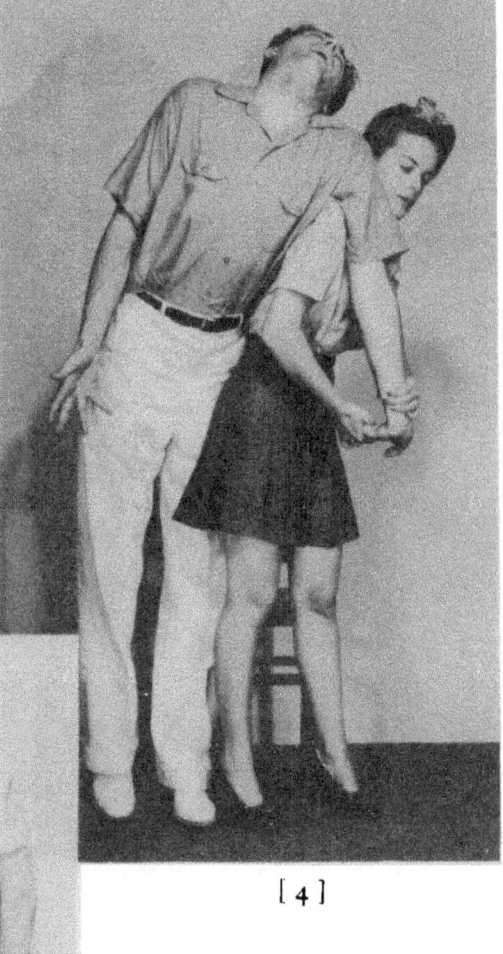

[4]

[3]

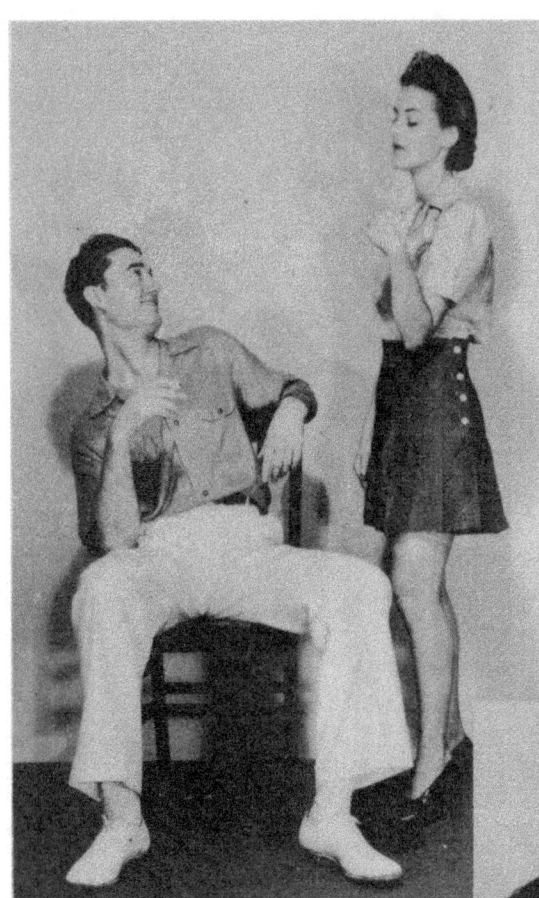

MANEUVER 4

A variation of the "lead-out" maneuver in which the "punishing thumb grip," as described in detail on page 16, is applied. This maneuver relies to a considerable extent on speed, dexterity, and the element of surprise, and it will require a great deal of practice. Remember that very serious injury can be inflicted on your sparring partner in the use of this grip and do not put too much pressure on the thumb that you have imprisoned.

[4]

[3]

MANEUVER 5

A familiar pest is the handshaker who won't let go when the period of polite greeting has more than expired (1). The treatment shown may seem a trifle drastic for someone who is merely being "fresh." Perhaps it is, but this type of approach may lead to something more serious. To break loose, twist your body *toward* the hand you

[1]

[2]

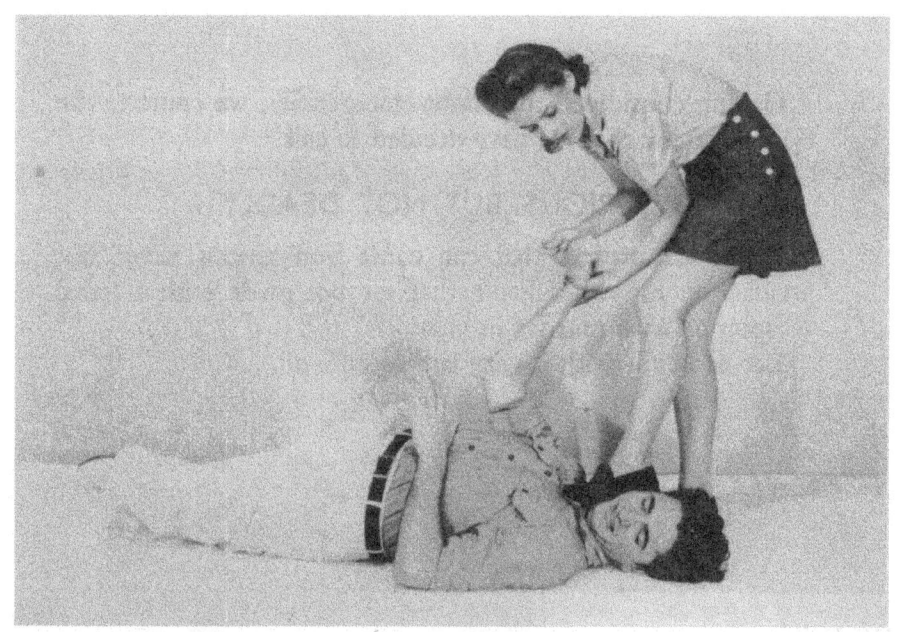

[4]

are grasping, retaining your grip on the pest's fingers, and be sure to keep the hands down low. Turn so that your back is to him (2). Reinforce your grip by grasping the offending arm at the elbow and throw him to the ground (3). You will be able to do all kinds of things to him at this point (4), if you so desire. Your elbow-gripping hand may be shifted to a little-finger grip (see page 16 for grip), which will place him completely in your power, and he can be finished off with a kick behind his ear or a foot on his Adam's apple.

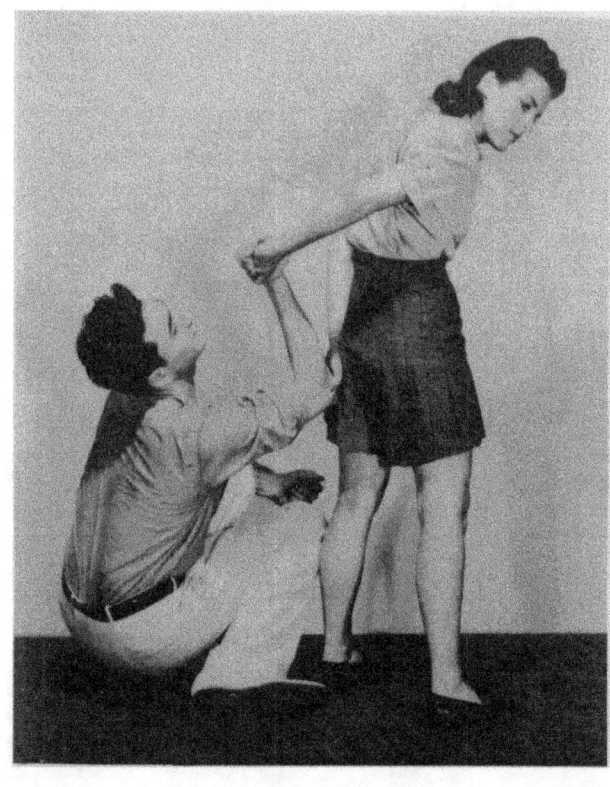

[3]

Having considered the minor emergencies, we come to the class of attack that we have decided to call

SERIOUS BUT NOT DEADLY

These are attacks that can cause you serious harm, but attacks, on the other hand, that are not made with a lethal weapon or with murder in view.

Let us begin with a very simple cure-all.

[1]

MANEUVER 6

The attack here may have been made in any one of a number of forms. It may have been a grab or reach for you, or intended as a blow or shove. In this simple defense, grasp your attacker's left wrist with your right hand from the inside and, at the same time, draw your right leg back (1). Pushing out and down on the wrist you hold, swing your leg through a complete arc as shown (2). Be sure to *follow through*. This is a lift not a kick. Your opponent will land on his back (3), and can be put completely out of the picture by one of the finishing blows.

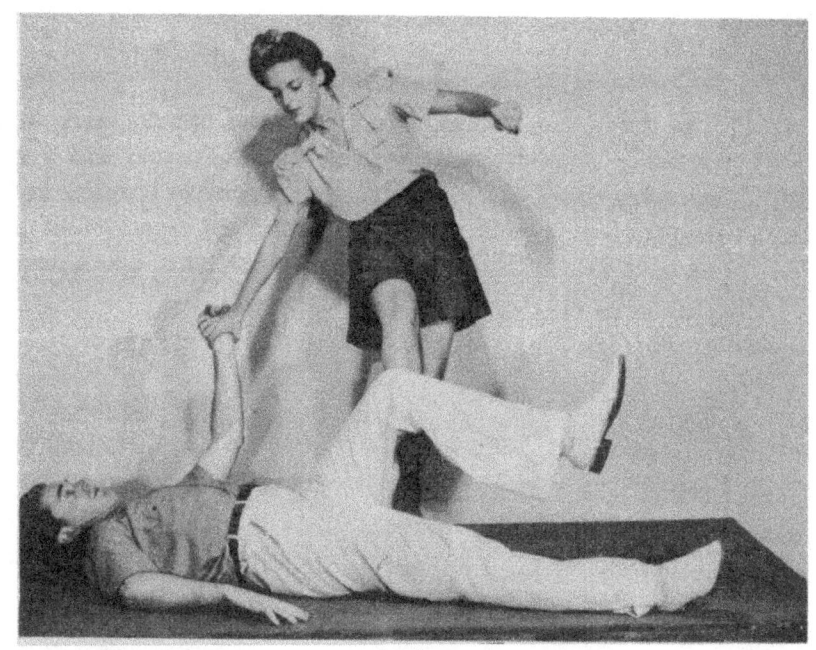

[3]

[2]

FRONTAL ATTACK

In defending yourself from a frontal attack, there is one factor in your favor—a moment of anticipation and a split-second opportunity to get yourself set and in balance. In that moment you can spread your feet apart slightly and poise yourself to meet your assailant. Do not tense up. Relax and keep your eyes open and on his hands.

GRABS

MANEUVER 7

To defend yourself from this two-handed grab, place your right hand on the inside of your attacker's right

[1]

[2]

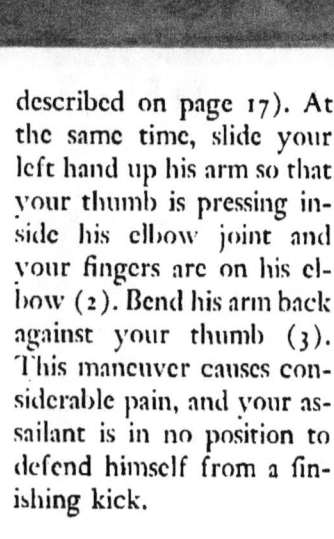

arm and grip the same arm from the outside with your right hand and obtain a "*wrist and thumb lock*" (grip described on page 17). At the same time, slide your left hand up his arm so that your thumb is pressing inside his elbow joint and your fingers are on his elbow (2). Bend his arm back against your thumb (3). This maneuver causes considerable pain, and your assailant is in no position to defend himself from a finishing kick.

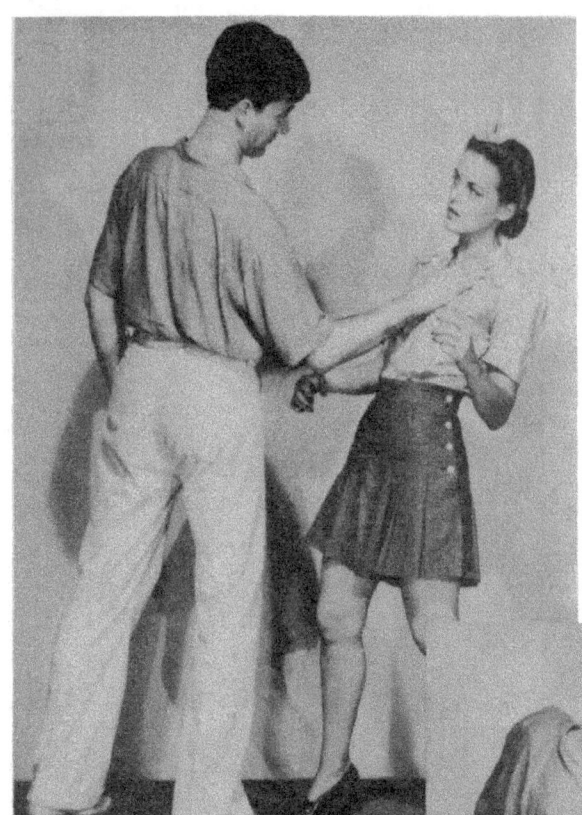

MANEUVER 8

A frontal attack with open palm toward you (1) can be met by grasping the attacker's right hand with your left hand, as shown (2). Your fingers should be on his palm and your thumbs should press between his knuckle joints. Twist his hand around as

[4]

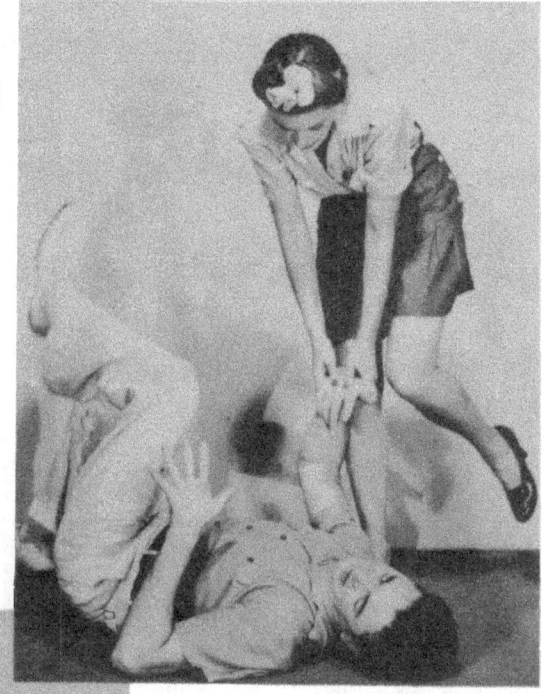

shown, and force it and his arm back and out on themselves (3). He can be laid on his back without difficulty. If circumstances merit it, he can be put completely *hors de combat* by kicking him behind the ear (4).

This maneuver is successfully accomplished because of its element of *surprise*—the fact that your initial grip is painful enough to distract your assailant's attention and leave no room in his mind to think of using his other hand to fight you off. In addition, the leverage applied to his arm, which is *locked against itself*, provides an excellent example of the leverage principles we have previously discussed.

[3]

MANEUVER 9

Another defense against a frontal attack with an open palm, similar to the one we have just described, is to grip two of your assailant's fingers in each of your hands (2). With your thumbs against the tip of his fingers you can bend the joints, forcing the fingers back and down (3). By

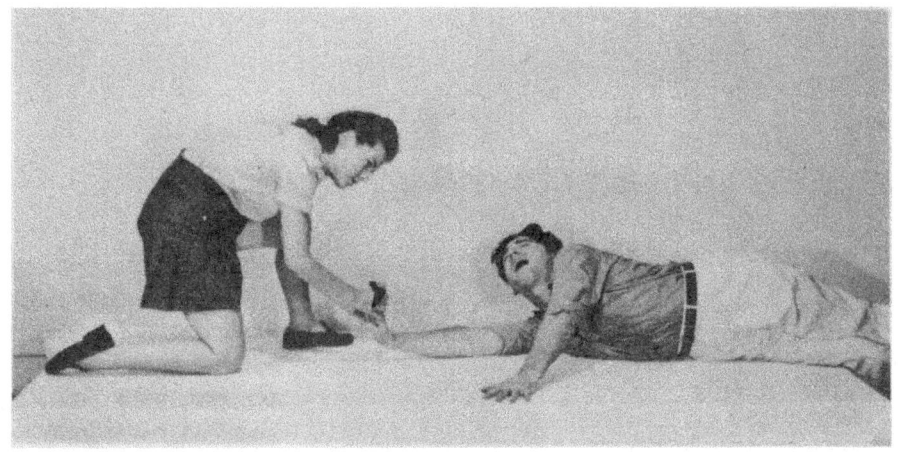

[4]

continued pressure he can be stretched out on the floor (4), and finished off at your leisure. You must remember, however, to back away to prevent his reaching for your legs as he goes down. The success of this maneuver relies almost wholly on the great pain you are inflicting by your finger grip.

[3]

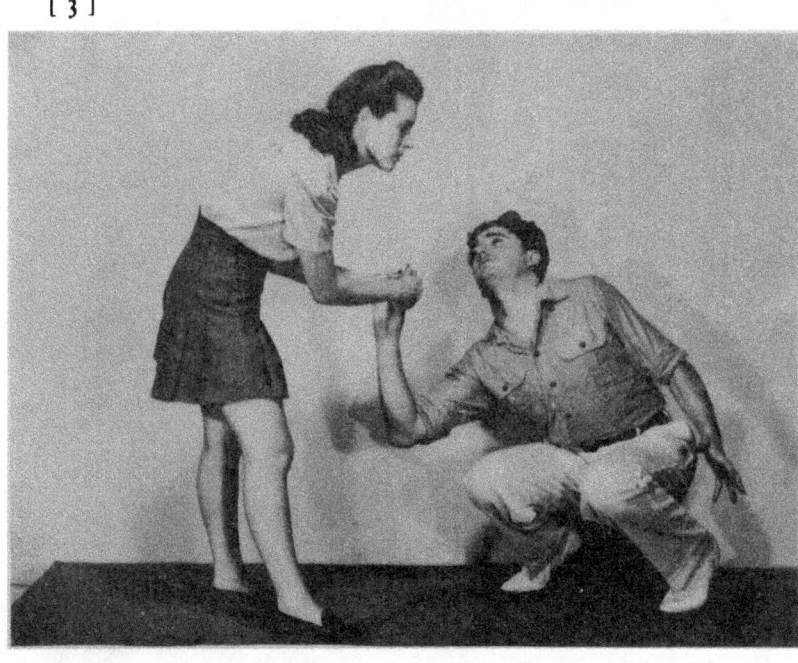

MANEUVER 10

An attack made from the front at about the level of and in the manner of an attempted left-handed handshake is countered as follows. Grasp two or three fingers of your assailant's left hand with your right as shown (2), and apply the back-handed finger grip

(3) described on page 17. Carry your forearm well over his arm, so that *your* wrist is over his wrist, and pull his fingers in, pressing down on his wrist. This causes him great pain, and you can exert *sufficient leverage* to force him down as shown (4).

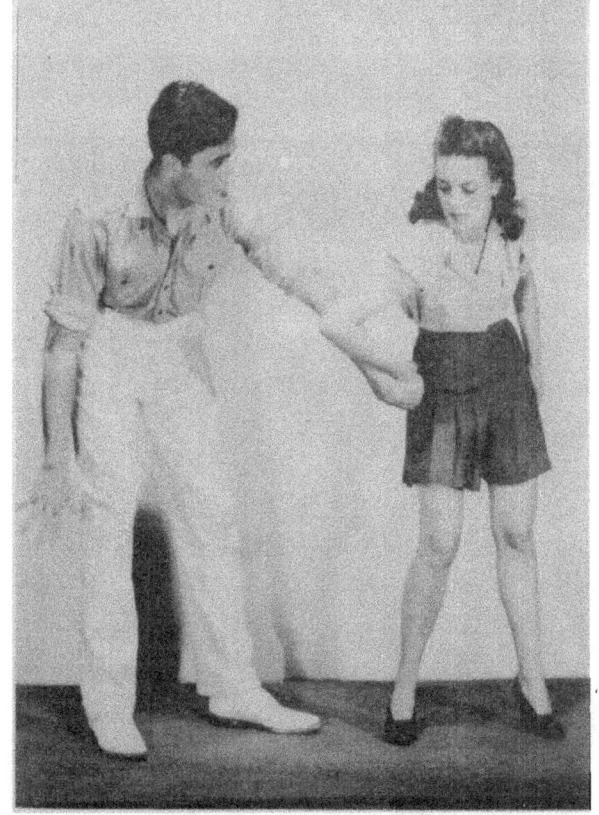

[4]

[3]

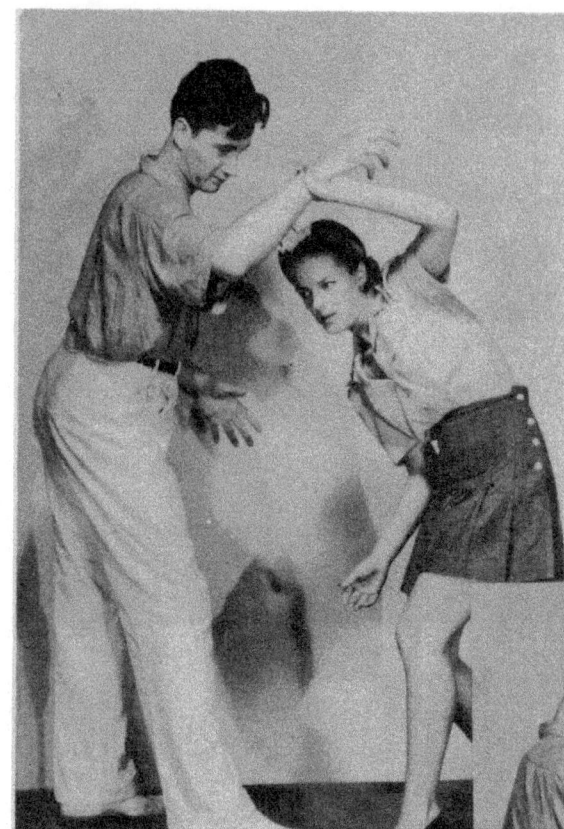

MANEUVER 11

A defense against the frontal grab shown is to parry the blow, bending your right knee slightly (1). From this *semi-crouch*, shove upward with your left hand (2), the heel of your palm under your assailant's chin. As you straighten up, put your left leg behind him, locking his right leg against it with your right hand, and continue the pressure on his chin (3). He's in for a crash-landing. Once on his back he is wide open for a finishing blow or an ankle twist (4). The ankle twist can severely injure his leg muscles. Be careful in practicing this one.

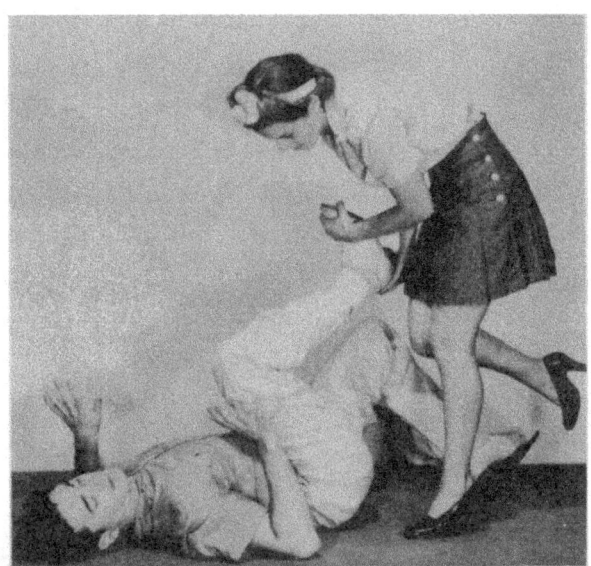

[4]

[3]

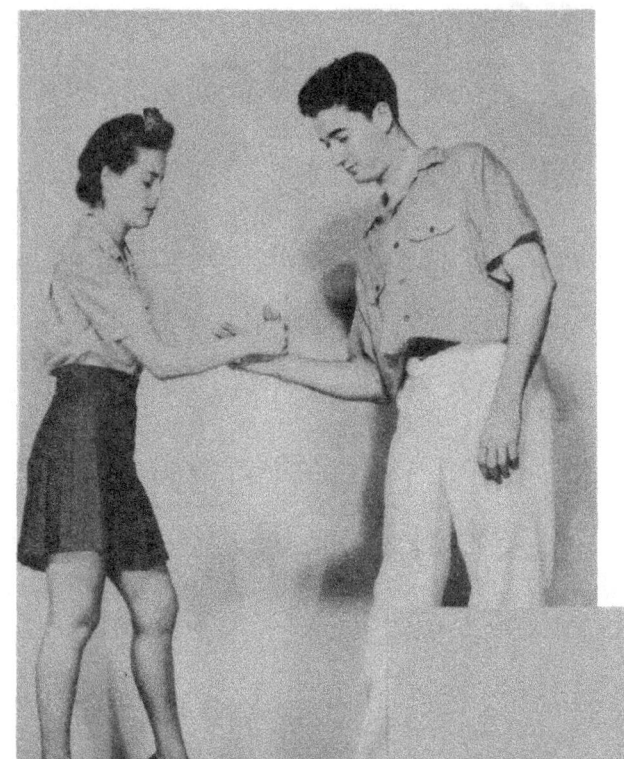

MANEUVER 12

To defend yourself from the one-handed grab shown above, apply a thumb grip with your right hand (1), as shown on page 15, and throw your assailant's hand in an arc to your left to swing him off balance (2). Extend your left arm full length and get hold of his

[1]

[2]

chin with your left hand and, at the same time, step in, placing your right leg behind his (3). He is bent over backward, and by keeping your left hand on his chin, forcing it back, you can lever him over your hip.

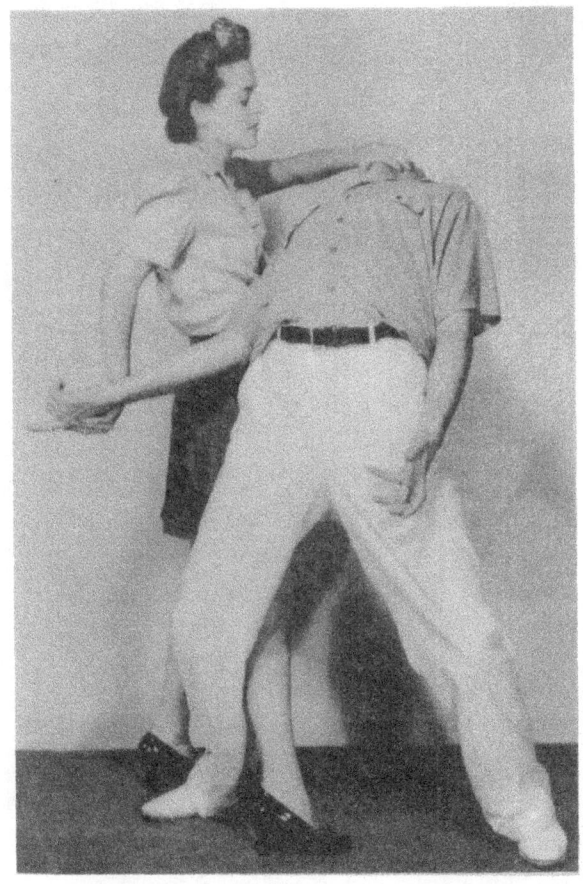

[3]

MANEUVER 13

The attack shown here is initiated by your assailant's grabbing the lapel of your jacket or the slack of your blouse or sweater (1). To prevent things from going further, apply the arm grip described on page

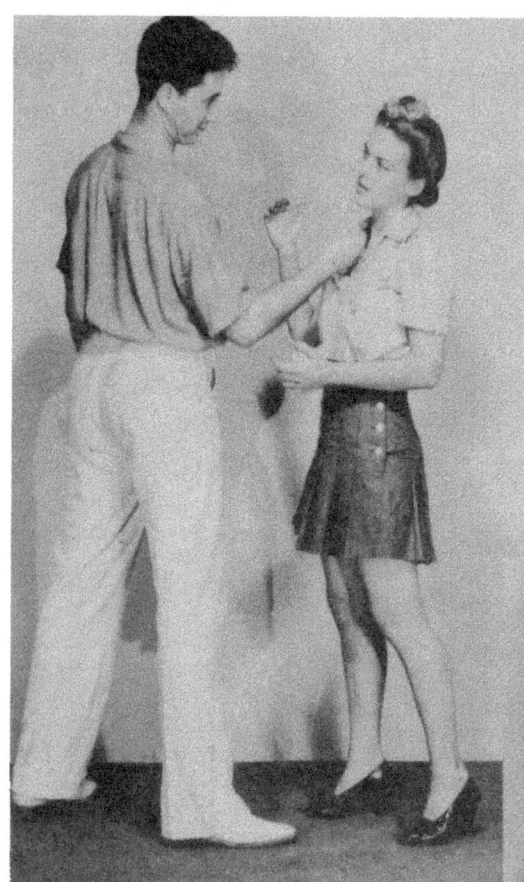

[1]

[2]

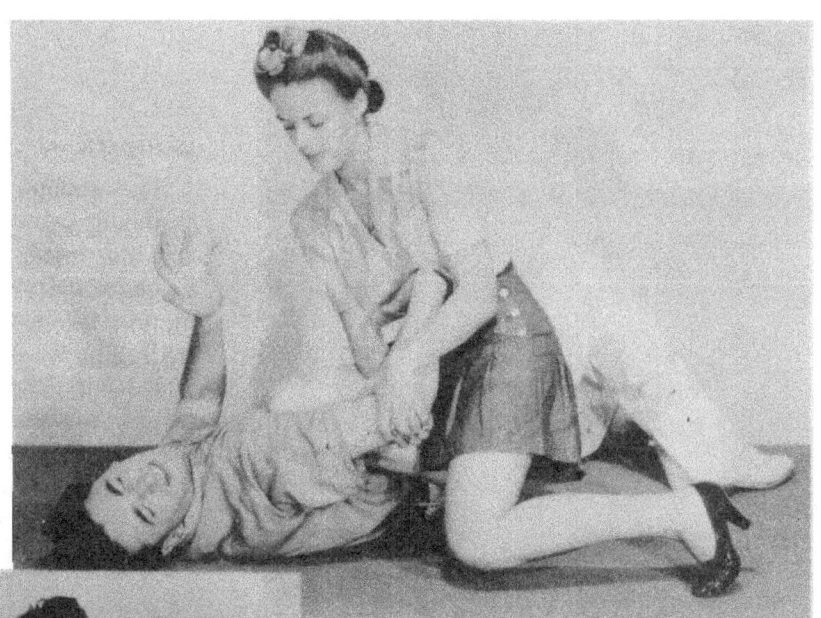

[4]

19 in detail. The grip not only renders the attacker helpless and causes him great pain, but it provides you with a lever, which, when you place your leg behind his, enables you to overbalance him and throw him over backward (4). When he is on his back it is an easy matter to use one of the "finishing blows."

[3]

MANEUVER 14

An attempt at purse-snatching (1) can be foiled and the snatch artist made to regret deeply his choice in professions if you deal with him as shown. Step well in and place your right leg behind his, and strike his Adam's apple a sharp blow with your right elbow (2). As you create this diversion, by attacking

[1]

[2]

a sensitive nerve center, you can drop your bag safely and then, grasping his right wrist with your left hand and continuing the pressure with your right elbow, lever him over your hip and lay him on his back (3). At this point one of the finishing blows is definitely indicated.

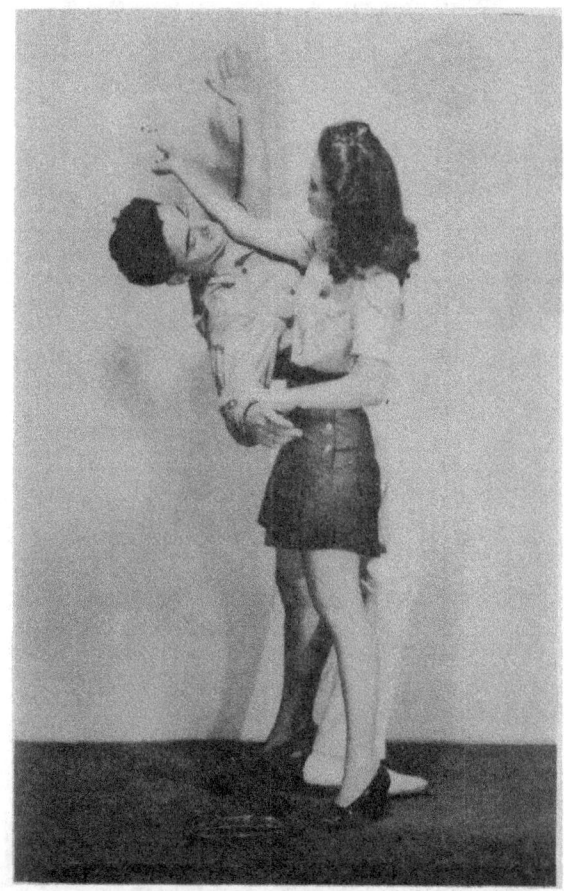

[3]

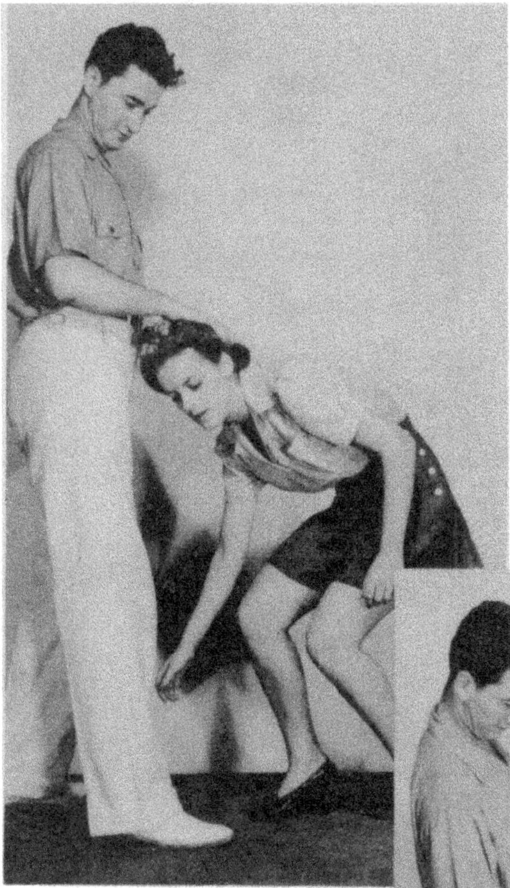

MANEUVER 15

The attack shown here has come as a complete surprise and in the form of a push that tends to force you to the ground. Do not resist—give with the force that is being applied (1), but as you go down, grasp your assailant's right ankle with your right hand (2) and place your left hand on

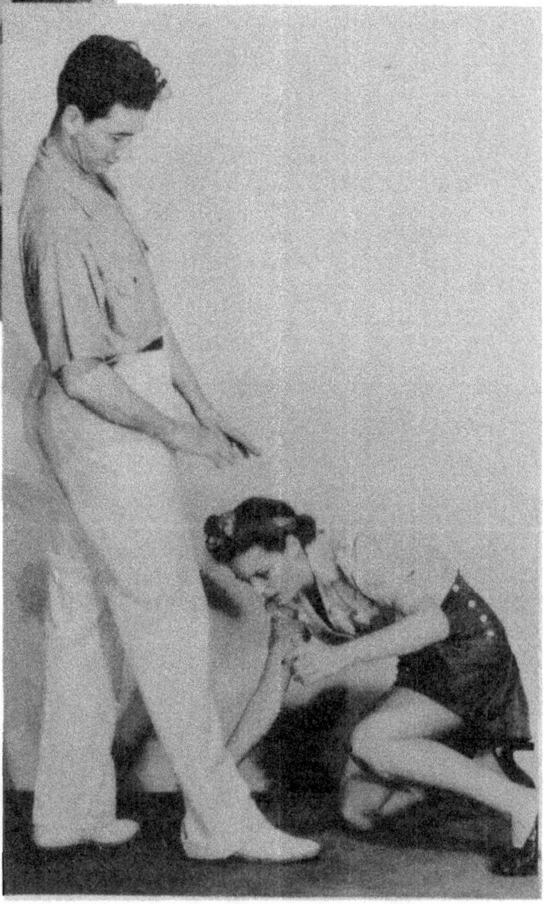

[1]

[2]

52

his knee (3). You have created a perfect lever, since his knee is locked against itself and he can easily be thrown over backward. At this point you can either deliver a cannily placed kick, run like the dickens, or tie him up with the knee grip shown (4).

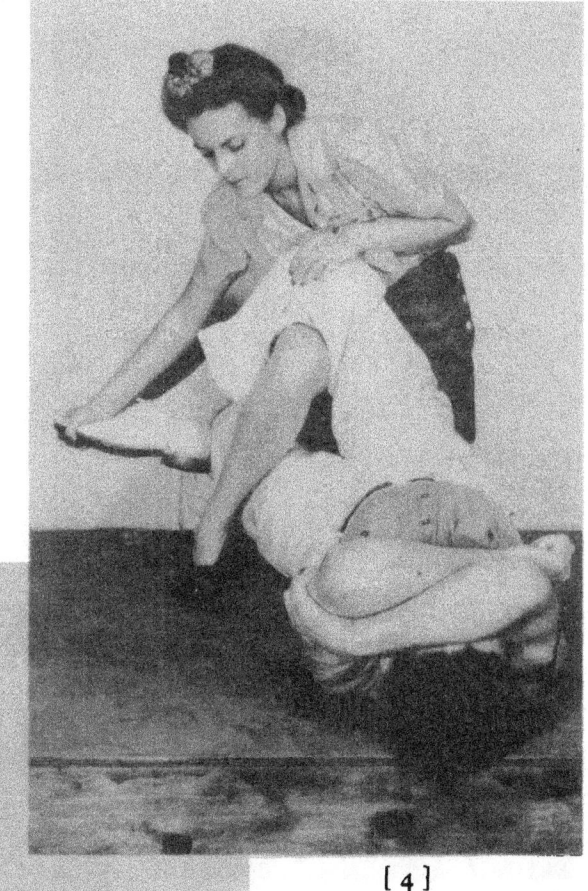

[4]

[3]

[1]

[2]

MANEUVER 16

It is for you to judge whether this (1) is a relatively harmless pick up or the first move in a more serious sort of attack. If you want to play safe, grasp his left hand with *your* left as shown, and pass your right hand over his arm and grasp your left. As you do this, duck in under him, turning your back toward him. He can be pinwheeled over your hip with surprising ease.

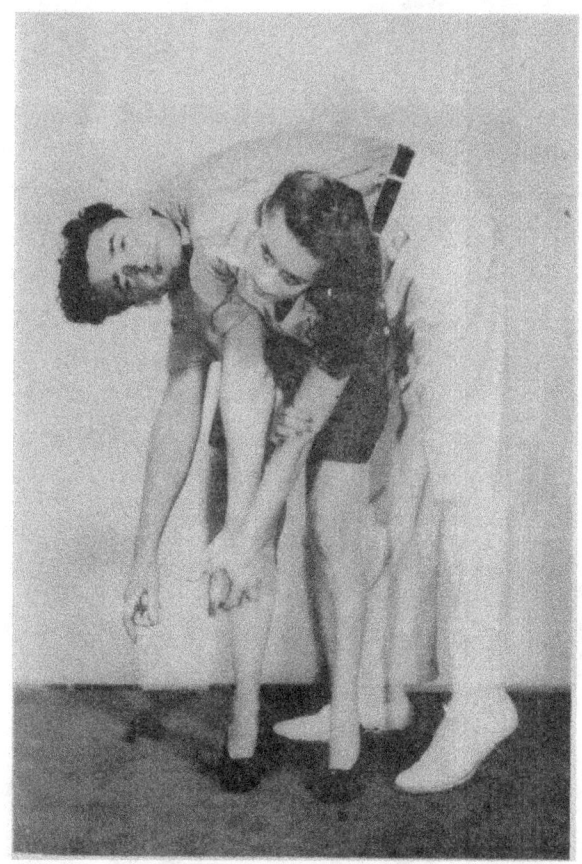

[3]

BLOWS

In the following sequence your assailant is shown as attempting to strike you a number of different blows that are well known in boxing circles. You will find the Combato defenses infinitely more effective against them than the boxer's would be. Your assailant in all these "clenched-fist" attacks is out to hurt you. Have no feeling about using a finisher on him.

MANEUVER 17

Your assailant is delivering what is known to the boxer as a "right cross." It is a blow with his right

[1]

[2]

[4]

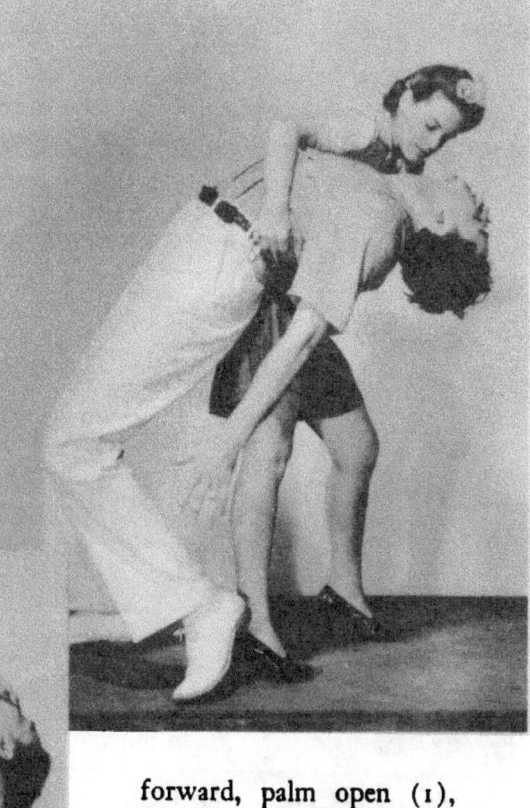

hand that is hooking in toward you from your left side. To counter it, parry, thrusting your left hand forward, palm open (1), until the heel of your hand is under his chin and your fingers are in his eyes (2). Step in as you do this, grab him around the waist with your right hand, slapping him hard to the left kidney, and brace your right leg behind his (3). By continuing the pressure on his chin you can overbalance him with your hip as a fulcrum and easily lay him on his back (4).

[3]

[1]

MANEUVER 18

In this defense against a right-handed blow, the force of the blow is taken on your right forearm (1). Turn to your right, grasping your assailant's wrist *from above* with your right hand and thrust your left

[2]

hand under the arm you are holding and grip the back of his neck
(2 and 3). You can do about as you wish with your attacker
when you have applied this modified version of what is known
to wrestlers as a "half nelson" (3). You can use whatever finishing
blow or grip you choose, or hold him till help comes.

[3]

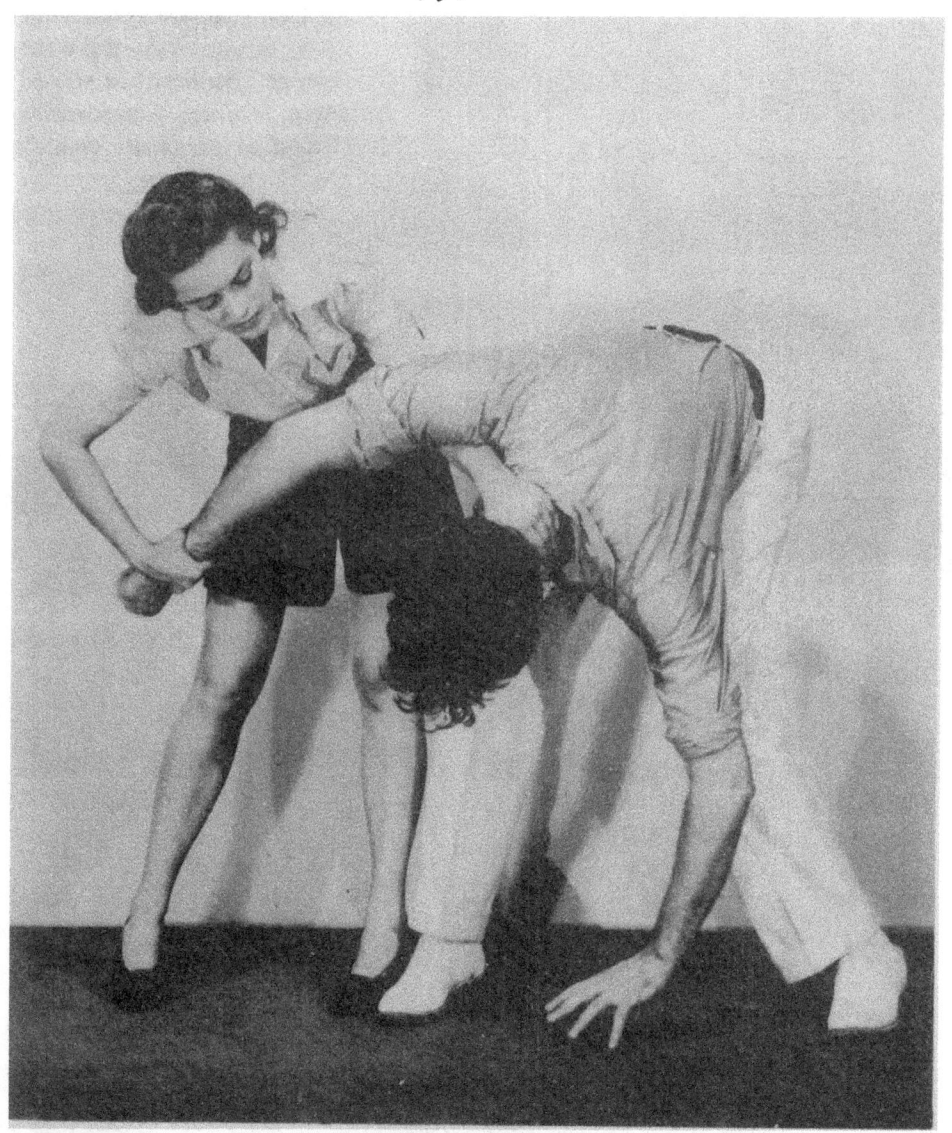

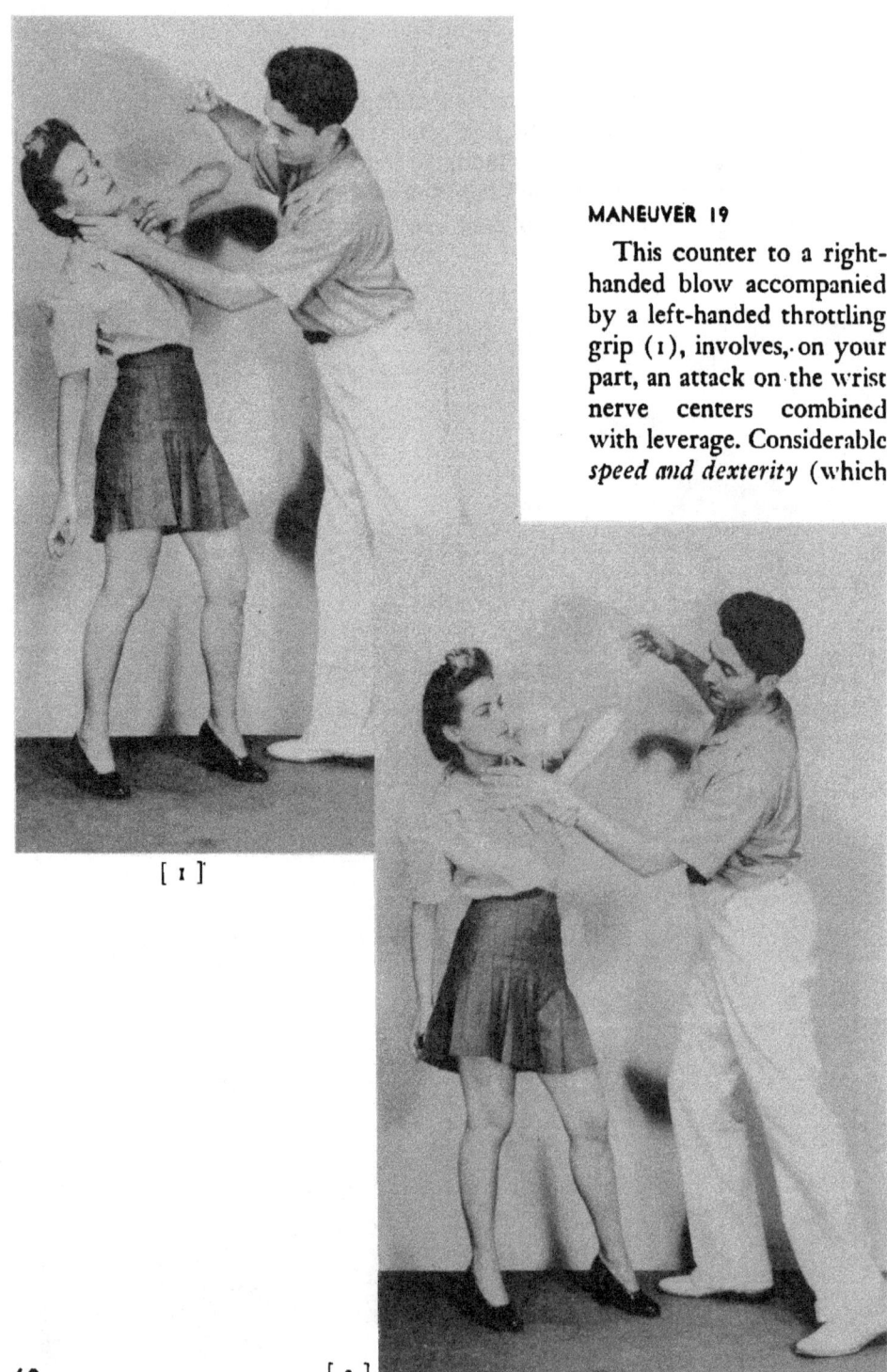

MANEUVER 19

This counter to a right-handed blow accompanied by a left-handed throttling grip (1), involves, on your part, an attack on the wrist nerve centers combined with leverage. Considerable *speed and dexterity* (which

[1]

[2]

[4]

in turn means practice) are required. You must intercept the blow by grasping the wrist of the hand that threatens you from *inside* (2). Your fingers should be on the under side of your assailant's wrist. Twist his

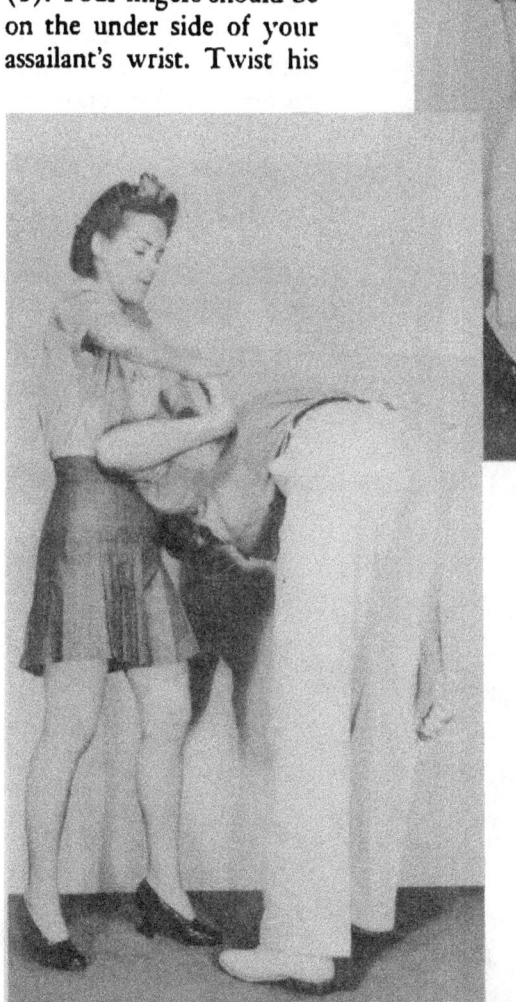

wrist toward you, and as this will create a diversion by causing pain, you can force his arm behind him, bending it back on itself (3), and form an arm lock that will render him completely helpless if reinforced with your free hand (4).

[3]

MANEUVER 20

An effective counter to a "right cross" (1) is to grasp the threatening hand from the inside (2). Duck under your assailant's right arm, retaining your grip, and bend over under his point of balance (3). You have made a perfect lever out of his arm, and by continuing to bend you can toss him completely over your back and shoulder (4). It is highly probable that he will land on his head with considerable detriment to his general health. Bear this in mind in practicing this maneuver.

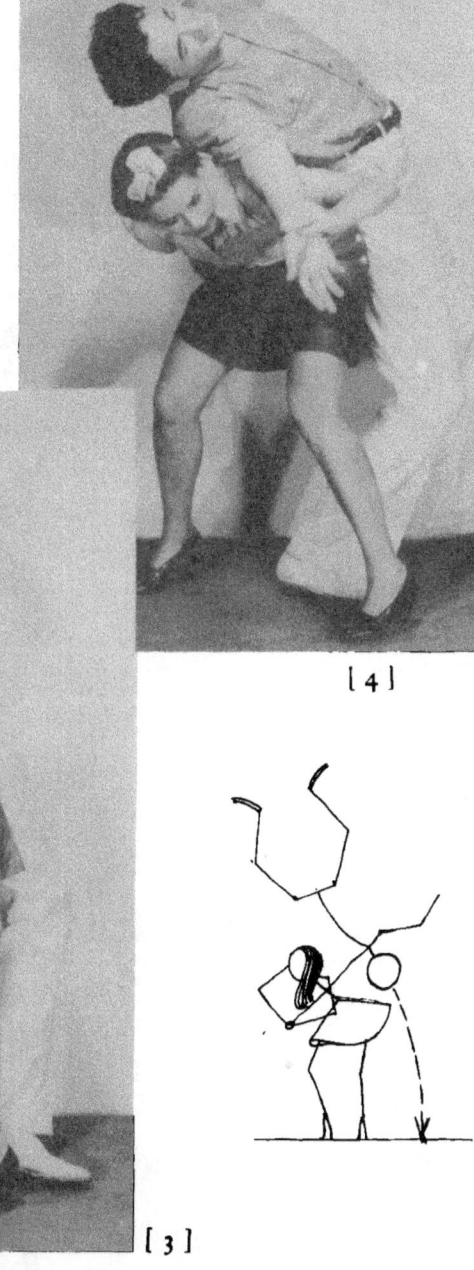

[4]

[3]

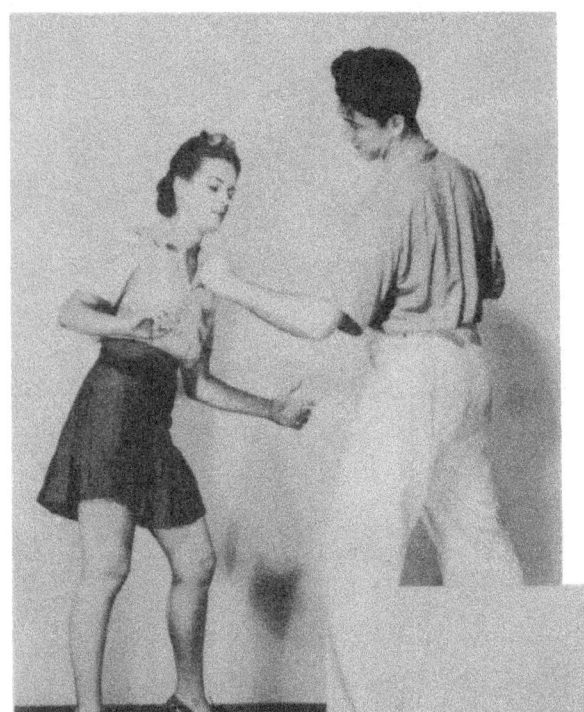

MANEUVER 21

This is a defense against a blow similar to that described in maneuver 20, except that the attack is made with your assailant's left hand (1). Your defense is to grasp his wrist from the outside with your right hand and twist it inward (2). Thrust his arm back as it gives at the elbow (it will, because of the pain you are causing), and double it up behind him (3). He will be in a completely helpless position, and you will have applied what, in wrestling, is called a "hammer lock."

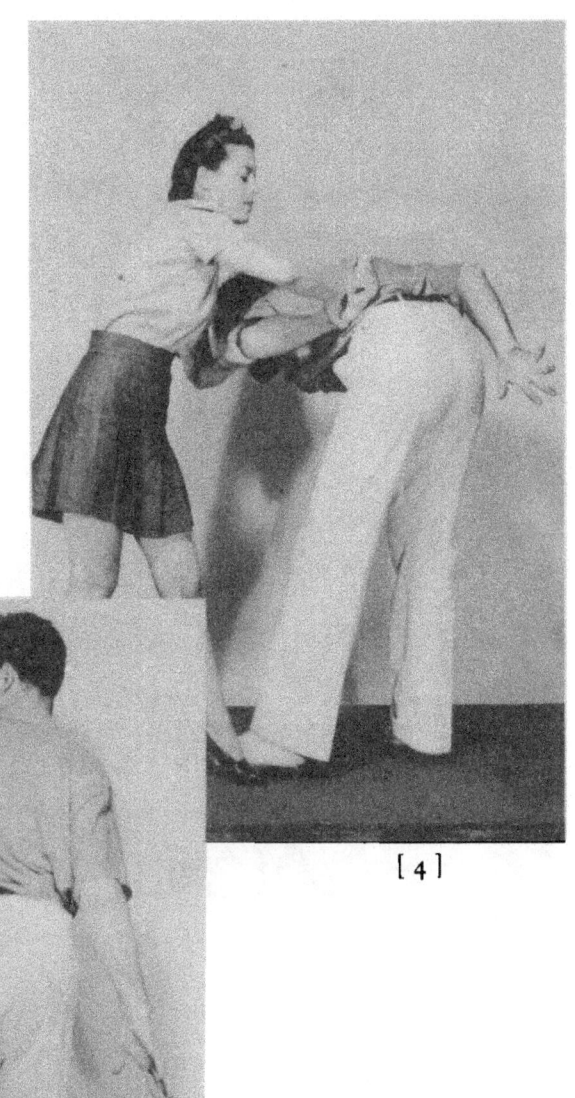

[4]

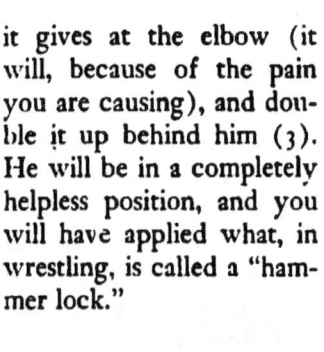

[3]

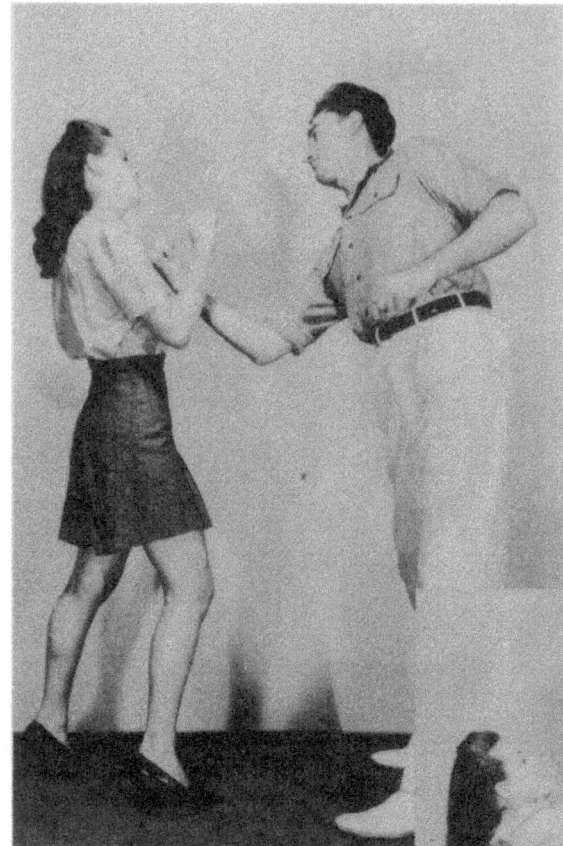

MANEUVER 22

An uppercut (1) is a lethal punch. It is a blow aimed at your chin from below and, if it connects and is properly timed and executed, it has laughing gas and ether lashed to the mast as anesthetics. However, it can be met, and the effort of making it can be turned against your assailant. Sway back slightly, let the punch go by, and grip the clenched fist as shown in detail (2). Ride up on it and let the force of the blow expend itself; then snap your attacker's arm down and bend his wrist in toward him (3). He can be brought to his knees and he is wide open for the finisher (4). The secret of this maneuver is the fact that you have made your assailant's attack throw him *off balance*. You are set and alert and, in order to avoid the excessive pain you are able to cause him with your grip, he has to yield.

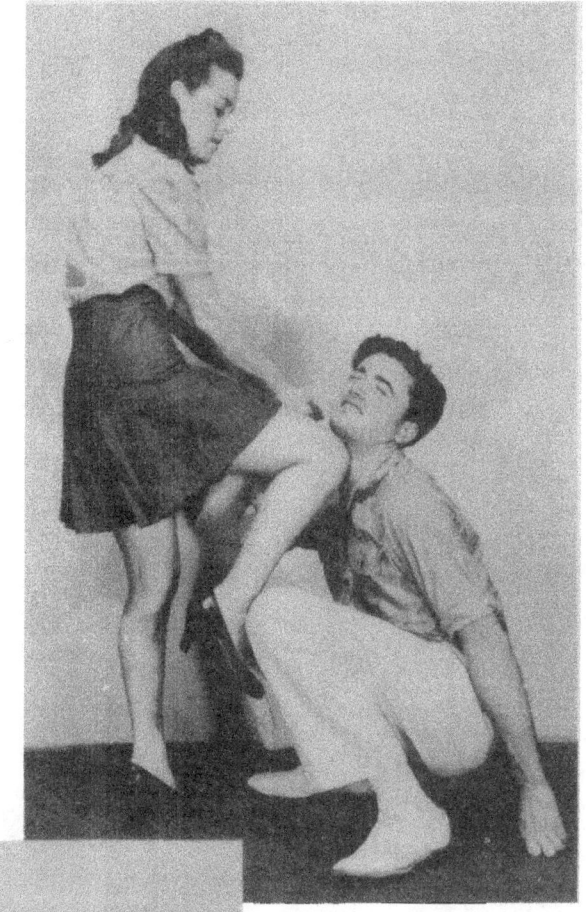

[4]

[3]

ATTACK FROM THE REAR

The attack from behind, illustrated below (1), has every appearance of being due to a mild fit of amorousness on your assailant's part, possibly because he is pictured here with a noticeably yearning expression. Appearances are deceiving, however, and this may develop into a most serious attack, particularly when you are alone. Hence rather drastic measures have been devised for meeting the situation. If you are convinced that the attack is only a flirtatious pass and help is near, use maneuver 1, page 25.

[1]   [2]

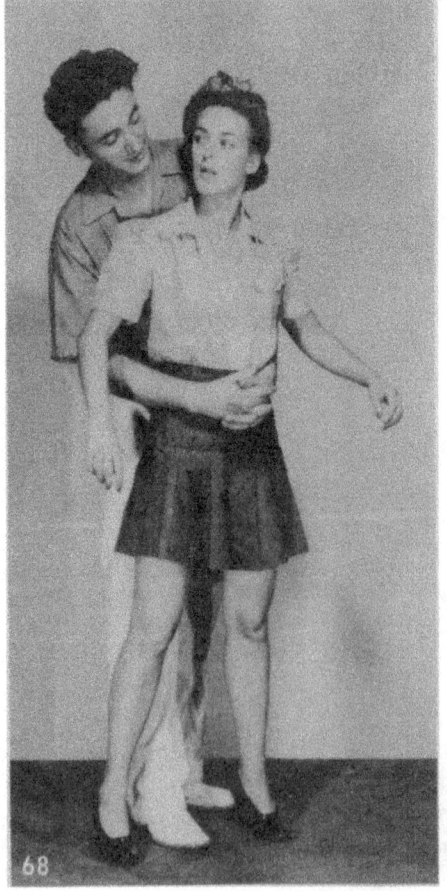

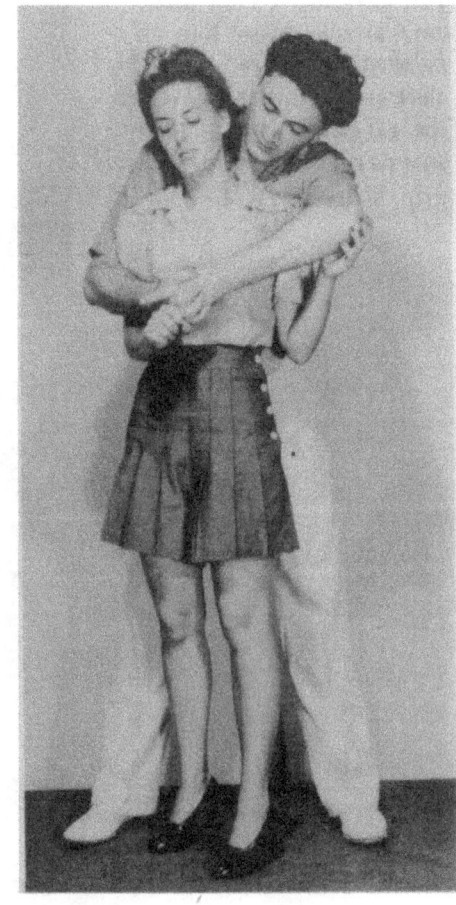

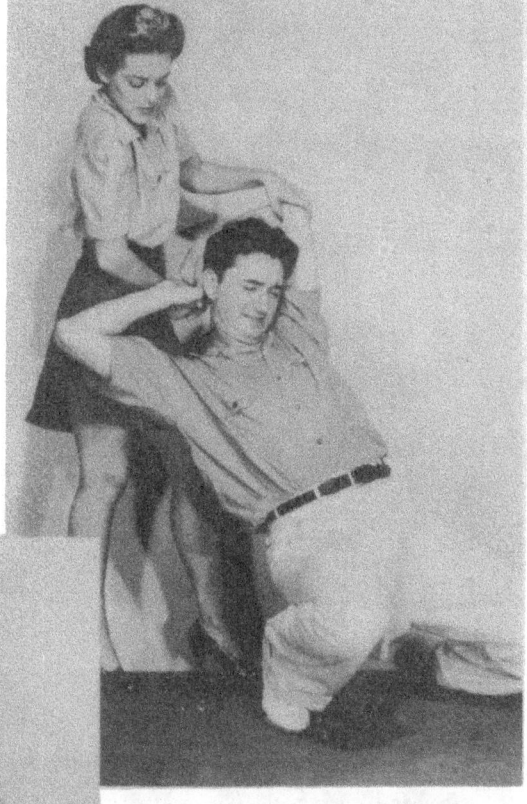

MANEUVER 23

Otherwise, with your right hand get hold of two of the fingers of his left hand and reinforce your grip by placing your left hand on his left elbow (2). Retaining your grip, turn to your left *to face him* (3). This will inevitably force him over backward to the ground (4), where he can be rendered helpless by a well-directed kick behind the ear, if this seems like a good idea at the time.

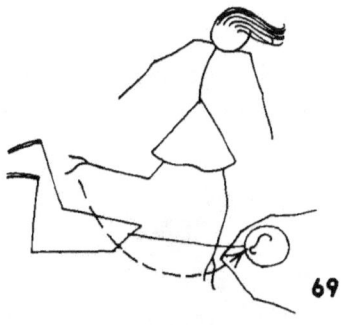

[1]

MANEUVER 24

Another defense against the waist-grabber (1), is to get hold of the little finger of his right hand with your own right hand (2). Turn quickly to your right, bracing your right leg behind his left leg, and grasp your right wrist with your left hand. Put your right shoulder under his right elbow to force it up and pull to your left (3). With your

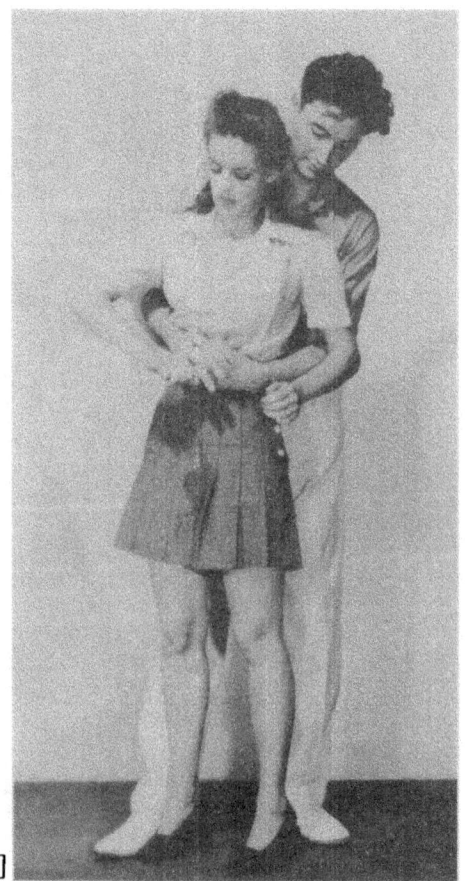

[2]

hip as a fulcrum, he can easily be *overbalanced* and thrown on his back. As an added twist, once he is overbalanced and on his way to the ground, you can release the grip you have on your right wrist and smash his Adam's apple with your left elbow (4). This blow attacks sensitive nerve centers and has a paralyzing effect.

[4]

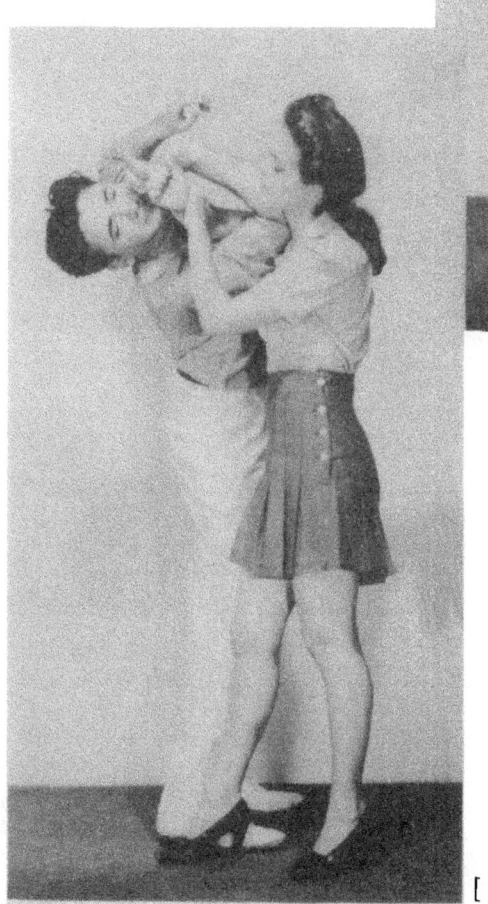

[3]

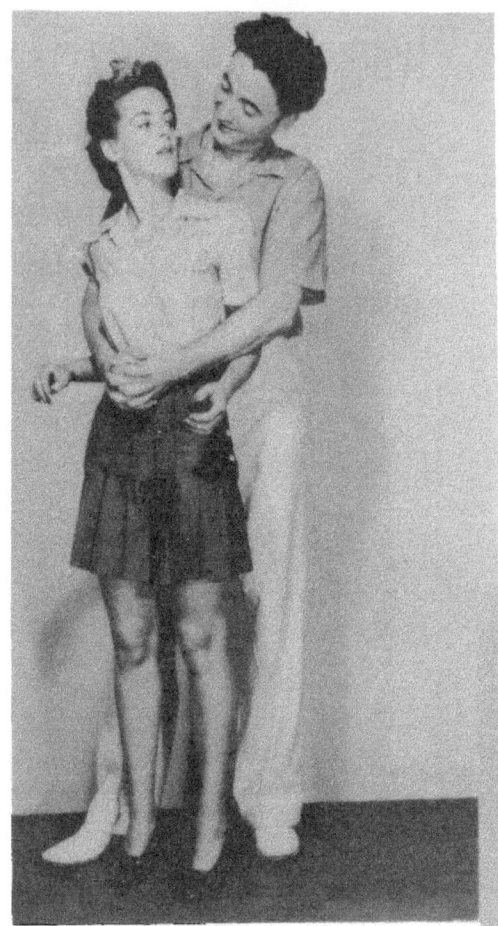

[1]

MANEUVER 25

Still another method of meeting the attack just described is to (1) lean forward and (2) grasp one of your assailant's legs at the ankle and straighten up. You are applying great leverage and he is bound to go over backward. Shift your grip on his ankle so that your right hand grasps his

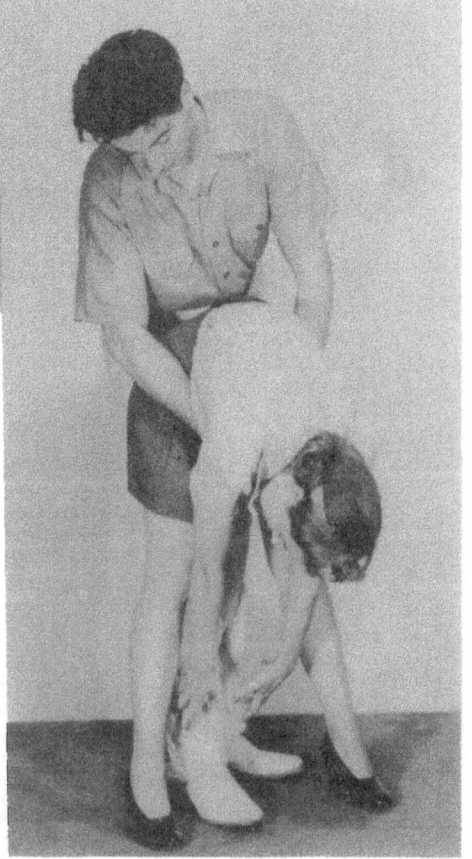

[2A]

foot as shown. Slip your left hand under his foot and grip your right wrist (3). You are applying a very painful and damaging toe hold. In practicing this maneuver, remember there is every chance that your assailant will land on the back of his head and land hard. Better use a mattress.

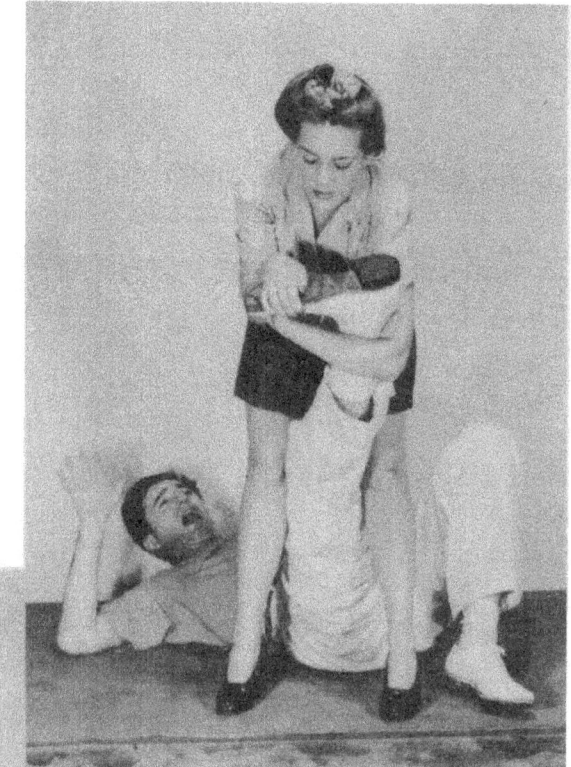

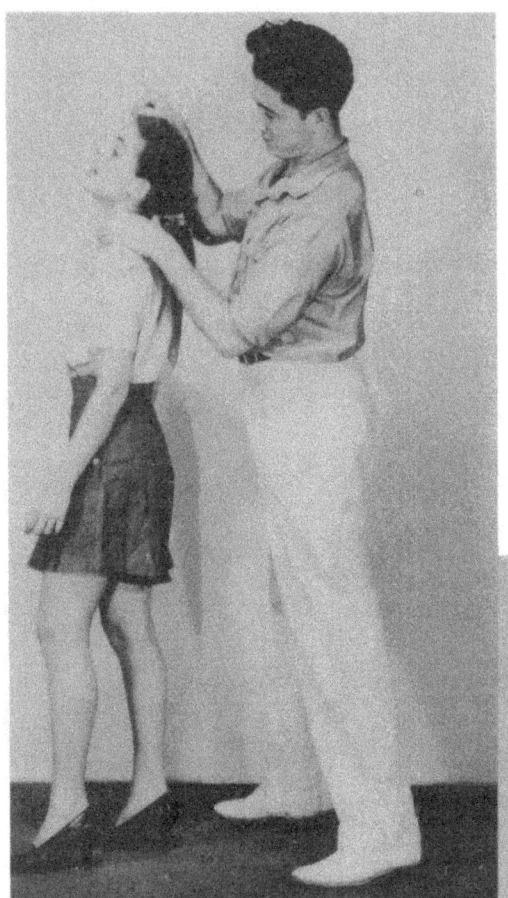

[1]

MANEUVER 26

If you are attacked as shown and your hair is in your assailant's grip with his other hand holding your arm or shoulder, *concentrate on the hand in your hair*. You'll need both hands to free it. To do so, grip his right wrist with your right hand, thumb on the wrist nerve center, and

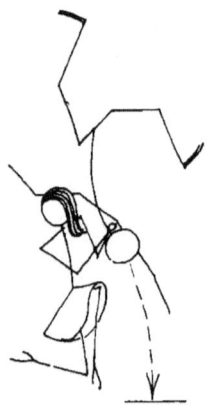

[2]

grip his hand itself over the knuckles with your left hand. You can cause him enough pain to break the grip on your hair. Turn his arm outward from the inside, and simultaneously pull it over your right shoulder. Go down under his point of balance and toss him to the ground. If there is any life in him after landing on his head, as he presumably will, apply the finisher that is shown.

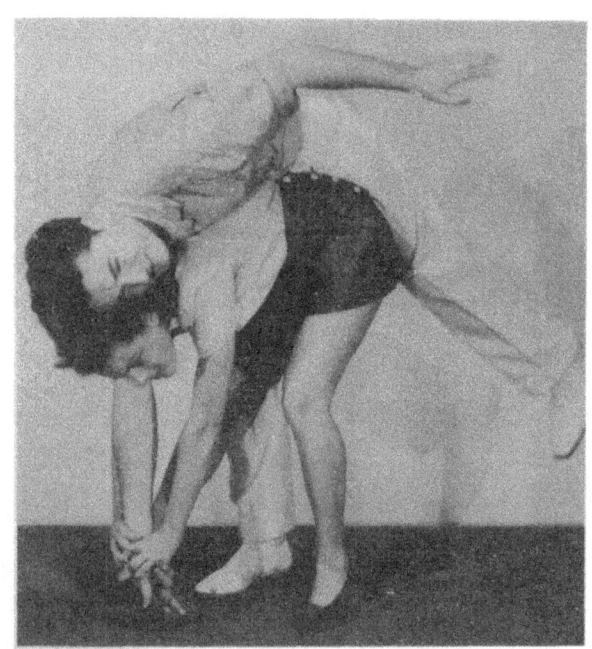

[4]

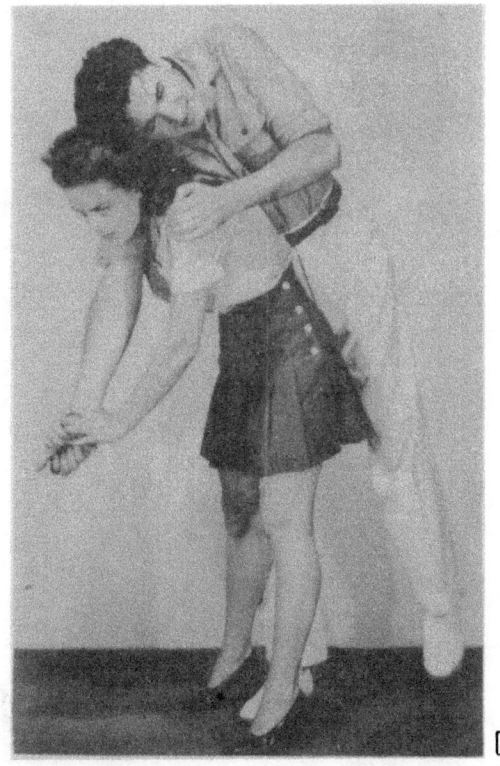

[3]

[1]

MANEUVER 27

The attack pictured (1) comes slightly from above and differs in that respect from the waist-grabs that have been shown in the preceding pages. To counter it, drop to your right knee and reach your hands up to grip your assailant around his neck with both hands (2). Get well below his center of balance and he

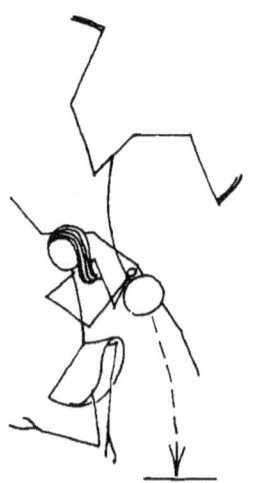

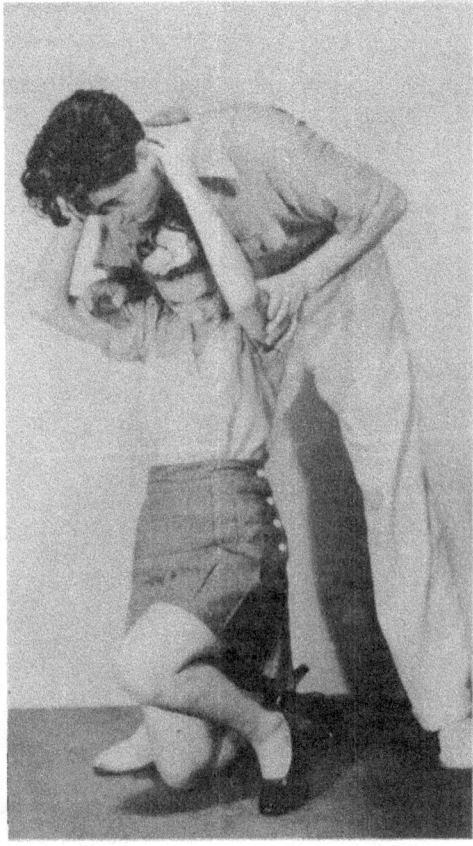

[2]

can be pinwheeled over your shoulder with surprisingly little effort (3). Once on the ground, he is a sitting bird for a kick to the temple or any one of the other finishing blows or arm locks.

[3]

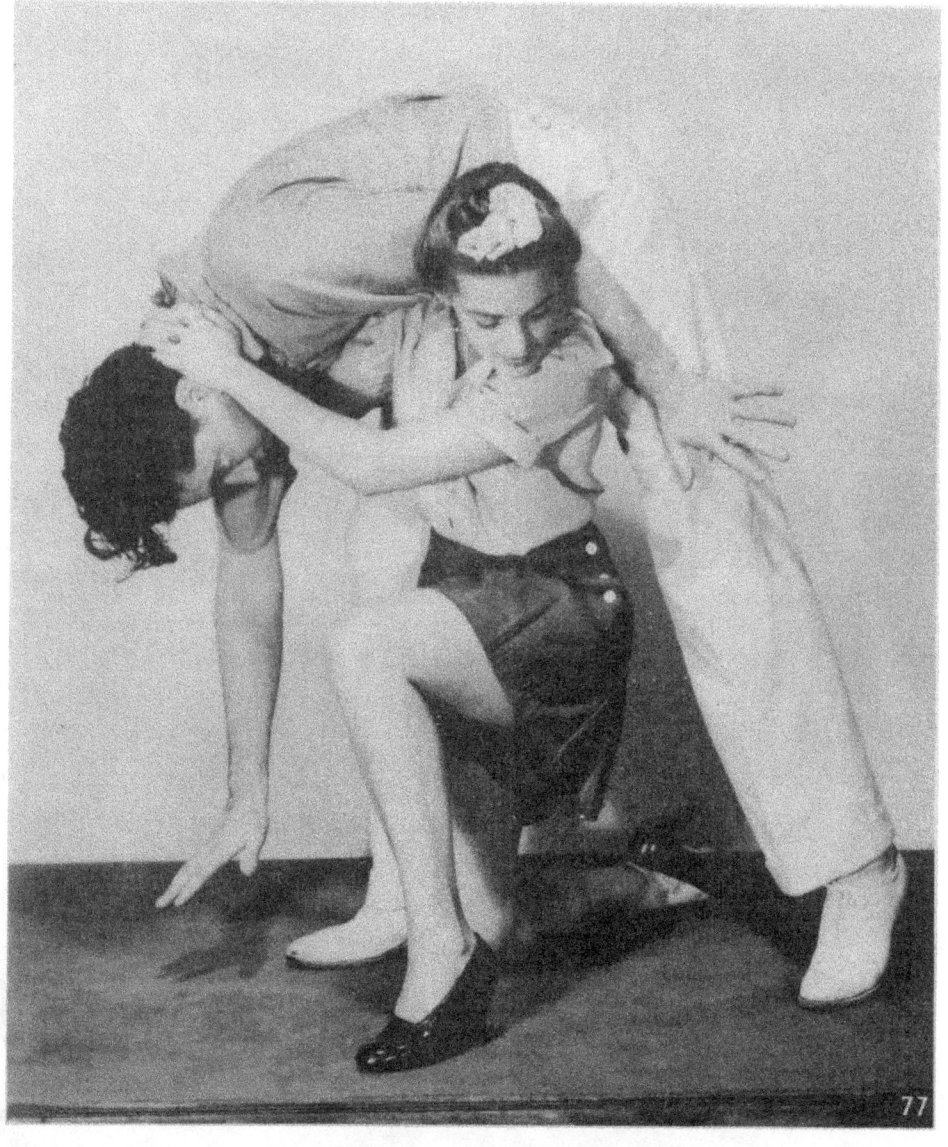

We now come to the category of attacks we have chosen to call

DEADLY SERIOUS

These are attacks in which your life is actually at stake, and the maneuvers that have been devised to meet them should be regarded with the utmost seriousness.

THROTTLING ATTACKS

[1]

[2]

 **OR**

[3]

MANEUVER 28

The element of surprise is on your assailant's side in the attack pictured (1). It is the "mugger's" attack, and the boy means business. Your best move is to relax and slump down in his grip. This will get you below his *center of balance* (2). Step off to your right and get your left leg behind him. Thrust your left arm out as pictured, and lever him over your hip (3). If his grip is not broken and he persists in holding on, he can be given a toss over your hip that he'll remember. Once on the ground he can be easily finished off as you can readily imagine.

MANEUVER 29

A throttling attack from the front (1) can be met by grasping the little finger of each of your assailant's hands (2). Keep your palms up. Force his hands outward from your throat, thrusting them as high as you can before bringing them down to his side with a twisting motion that tends to *turn*

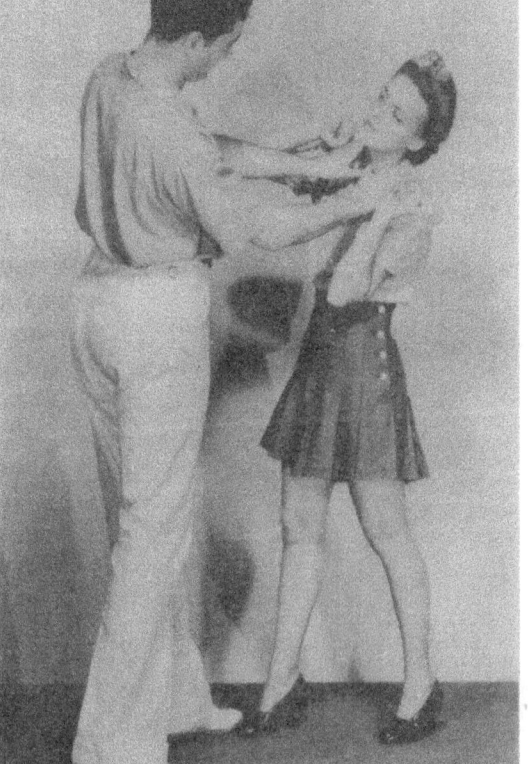

[1]

[2]

the palms of his hands away from his body (3 and 4). Bend over and thrust your head between his legs, retaining your finger grip (5). Continue to force your body forward and straighten up. He can be tossed over your back with surprising ease (6).

Two factors enter into this maneuver. The first is that the *great pain* of the grip you are using disconcerts your attacker and permits you to complete the maneuver. The second is that you are giving a living demonstration of the lever principle with your body as a fulcrum and his arms as levers, which accounts for the great ease with which the finale is accomplished.

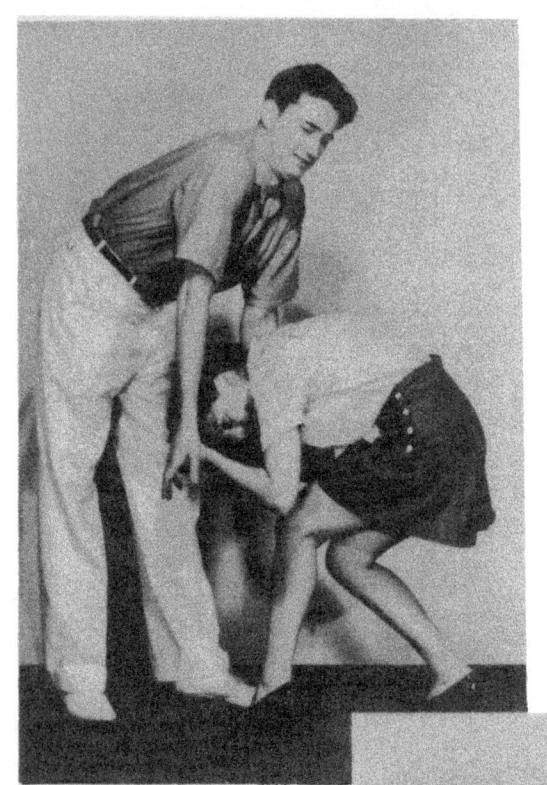

[5]

NOTE: This is an extremely dangerous maneuver for your sparring partner if carried to its conclusion, as will be obvious from the sketch. Better stop at the position shown in illustration 4. The rest is duck soup anyway.

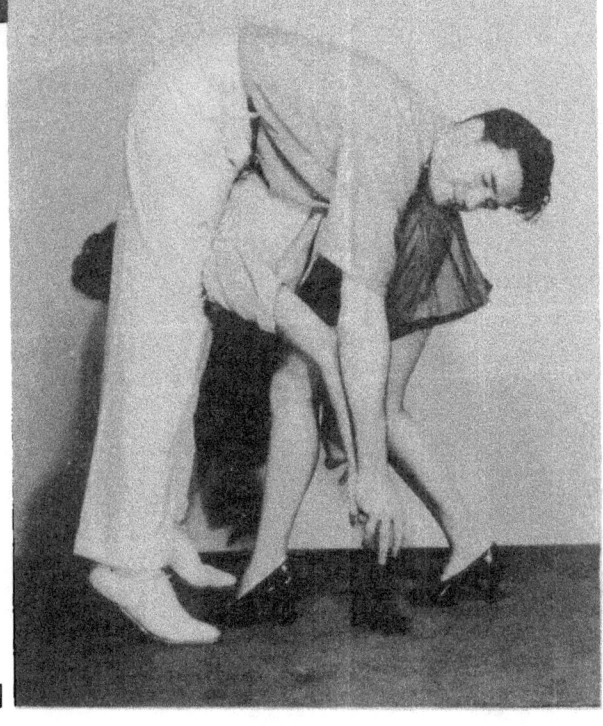

[6]

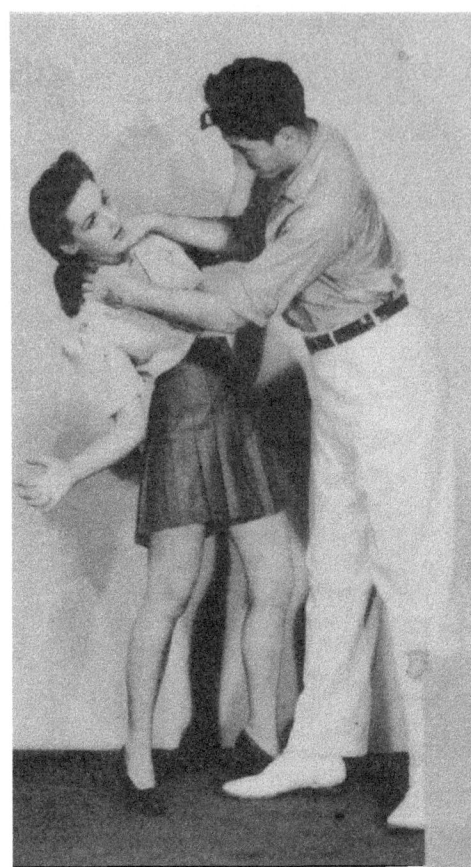

MANEUVER 30

Another method of countering a "strangle hold" such as the one shown (1) is to reach over your assailant's left arm with your right hand. Grasp that wrist with your left hand as a reinforcement (2). You have established a perfect basis for applying leverage. Bend to your right, retaining the grip you have secured, and you will not only break the strangle hold but will have your assailant in a position where he is in considerable pain and, to all intents and purposes, helpless.

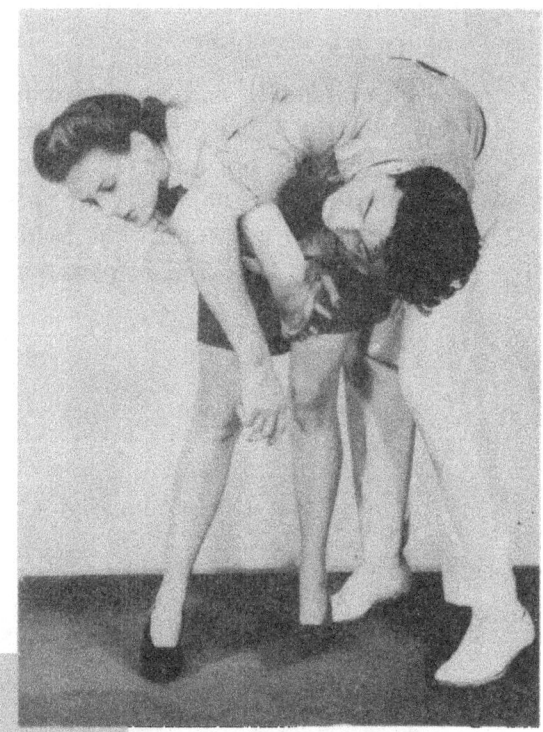

[4]

[3]

REVOLVER HOLDUPS

This obviously is to be classed among the "deadly serious" situations to which we have referred. If, by constant practice, you have not mastered the maneuvers shown, and are not absolutely certain of your speed and dexterity in their execution, do not resist. The holdup man *can*, however, be disarmed and rendered helpless.

(3)—your left thumb between his first and second knuckle joints. Bend his hand inward toward his body and, *using his arm as your lever,* force him over

[1]

MANEUVER 31

Strike the wrist of his gun hand with the side of your left hand (2), making a half-turn to your left. Grasp his hand as shown

[2]

[5]

[4]

[3]

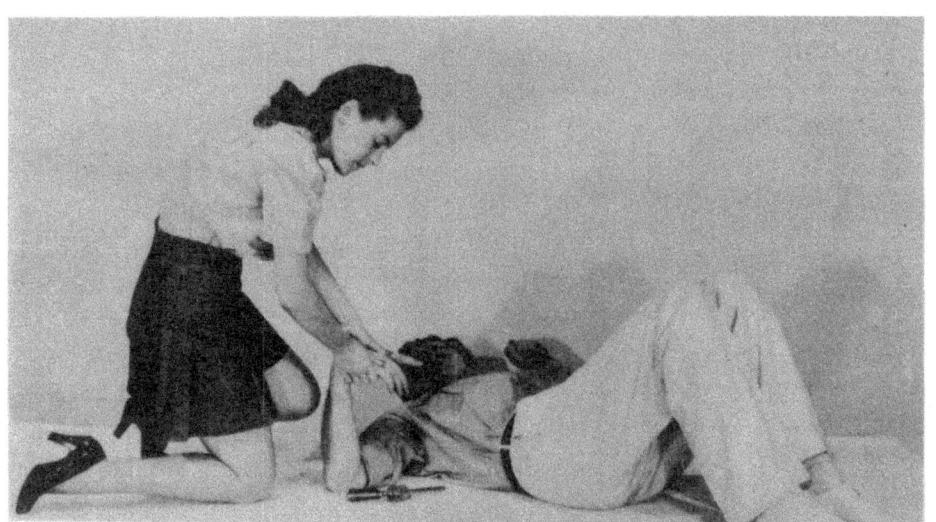

backward (4). Continue to twist his hand as shown, and he can readily be disarmed (5). Get hold of his gun as quickly as you can.

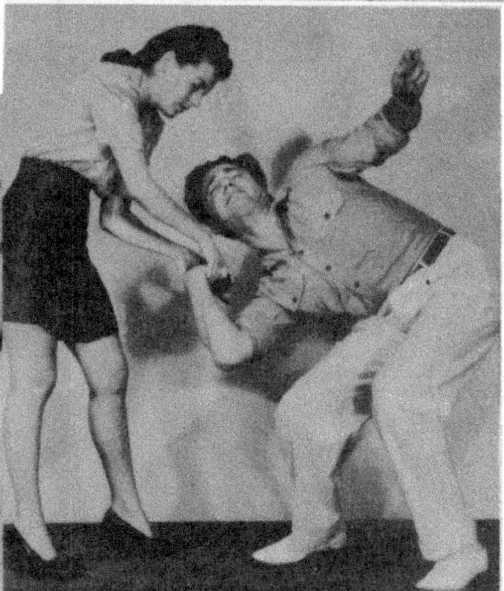

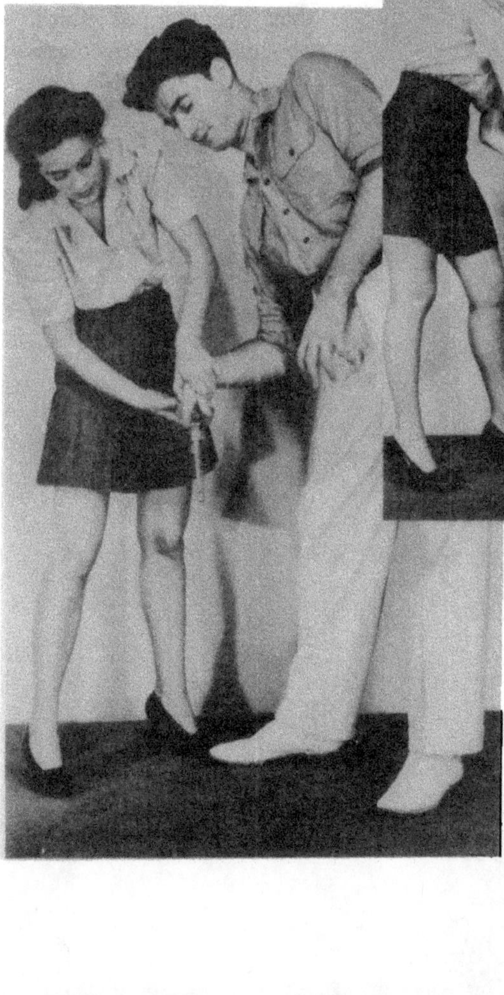

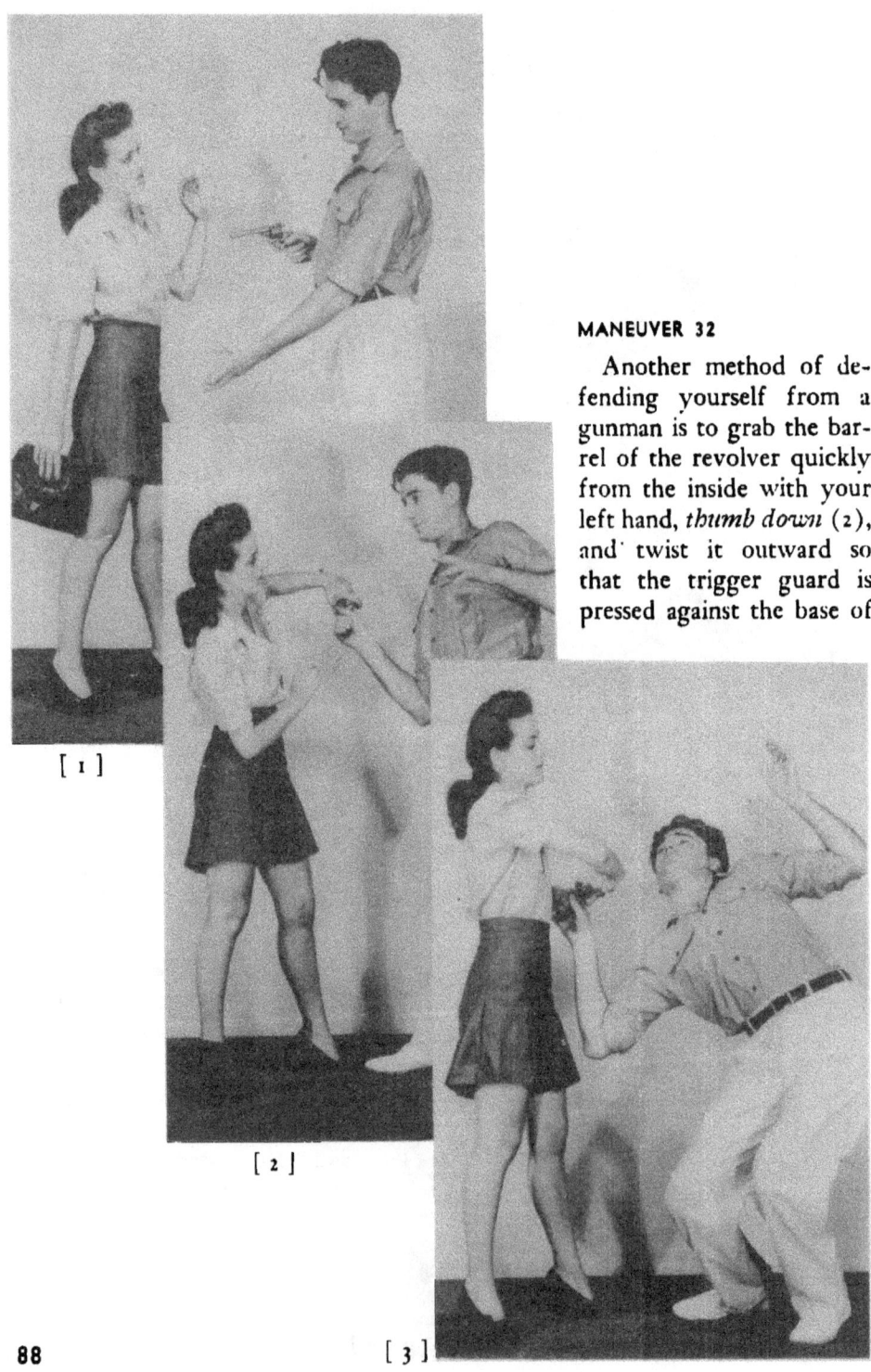

MANEUVER 32

Another method of defending yourself from a gunman is to grab the barrel of the revolver quickly from the inside with your left hand, *thumb down* (2), and twist it outward so that the trigger guard is pressed against the base of

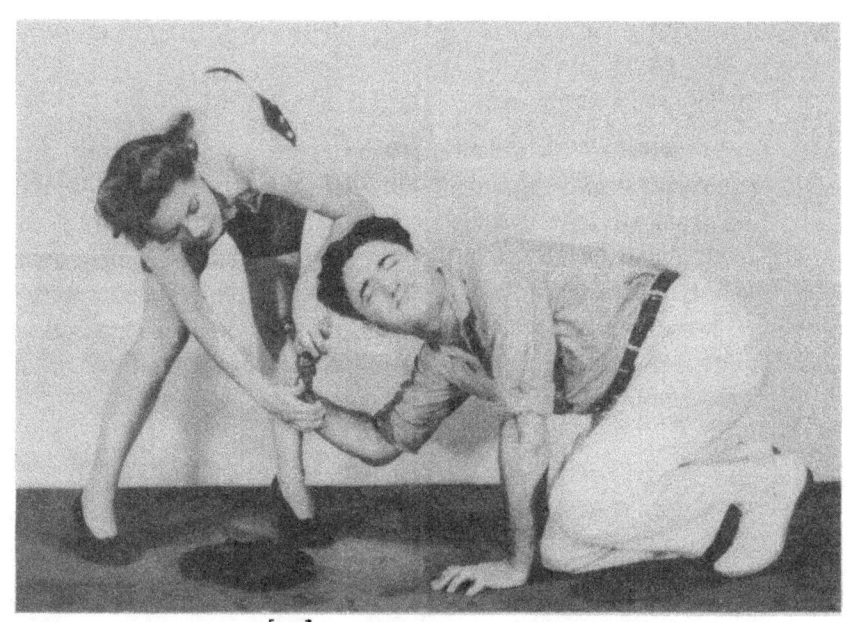

[4]

his trigger finger. It will not matter if the gun explodes here, as the barrel is turned away from you. Reach under his arm with your right hand and reinforce your grip on the barrel, continuing to twist (3 and 4). Your assailant can be turned completely around as shown and be rendered absolutely helpless (5).

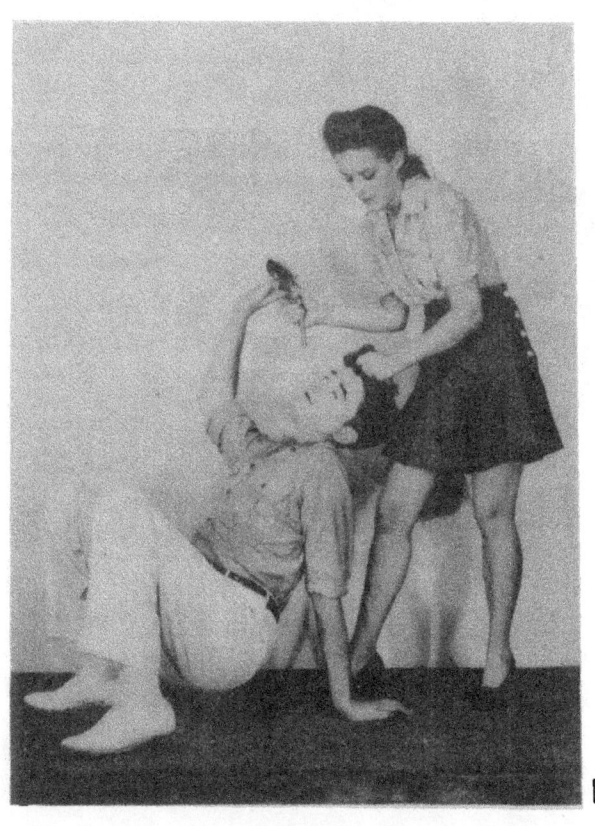

[5]

KNIFE ATTACKS

An attack with a knife can be even more terrifying than a gunman's holdup, and it should be, for the gunman is making a threat that can be defied or acceded to, whereas the knife artist clearly means business. The defensive maneuvers against this type of attack require considerable speed and lots of practice. Be sure, however, to practice them with a rubber knife, if available, or no knife at all, for the safety of all concerned.

[1]

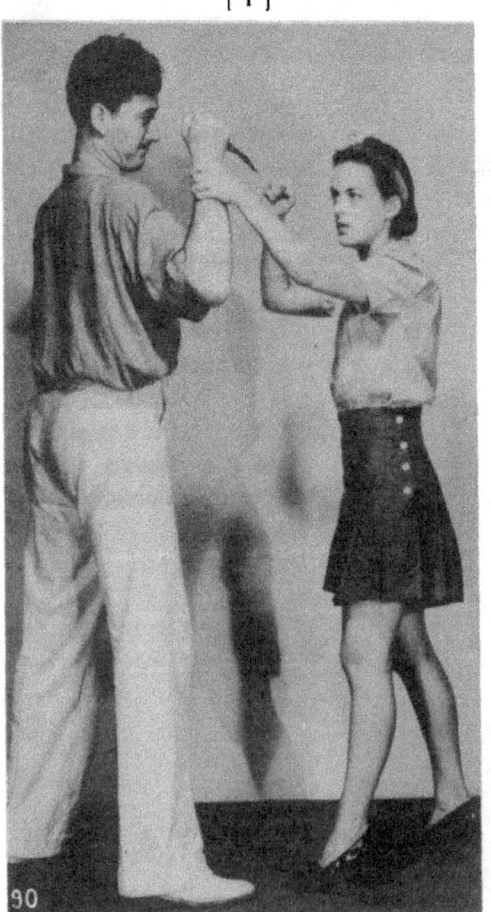

[2]

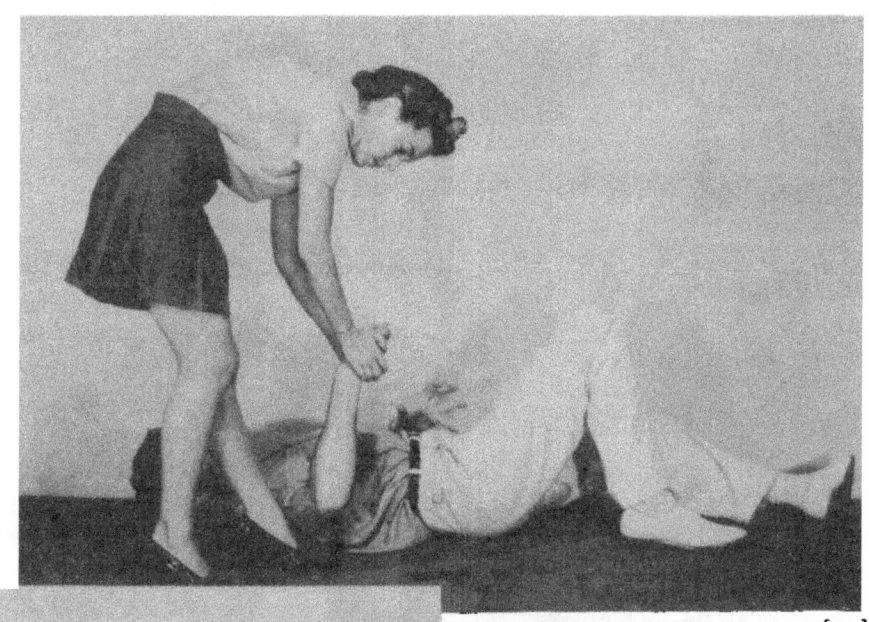

MANEUVER 33

To counter an overhand knife attack (1), grasp your assailant's wrist with your left hand (2) and, throwing your right arm over his elbow joint, twist his wrist, forcing him to turn his knife toward his own neck. Reinforce your grip by grasping your arm with your right hand, and, as you come to close quarters, thrust your right leg behind him (3) and, using your hip as a fulcrum, lever him over backward. As he starts to fall, shift the grip you have on his wrist to the handhold shown, your thumb pressing on the back of his hand. He will go down and probably stab himself with his own knife.

[1]

MANEUVER 34

The "upswing" knife attack that is shown here (1) bears the mark of the professional knife-fighter. This is the traditional attack by a man who knows his business. Your defense against it (and it better be good) is to reach over and around the knife hand with your left (2) and grip it with

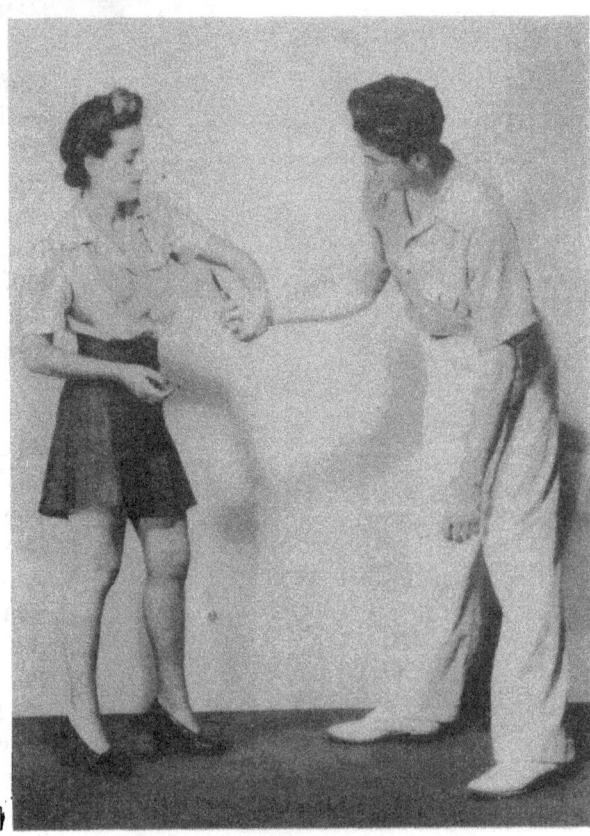

[2]

your fingers over your assailant's knuckles. Reinforce your grip with your right hand (3), the fingers of your right hand over the knuckles of your left. Now swing your attacker's right arm over and out as shown (4), and he can be thrown on his back and finished off at your leisure.

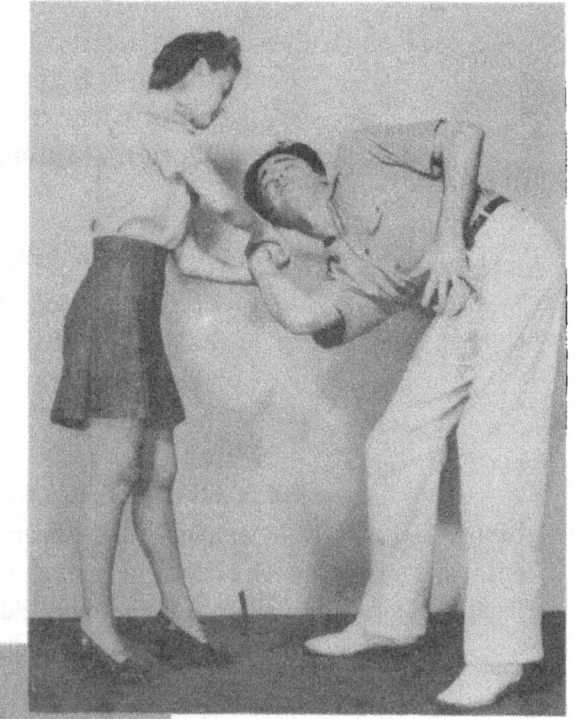

[4]

[3]

A Selection Of Classic Instructive Titles Relating To The Art Of
Pugilism & Self Defence
In Both War & Peace
Find our entire selection @ naval-military-press.com

ALL-IN FIGHTING
The distilled knowledge of W.E. Fairbairn, legendary SOE instructor in unarmed combat, and inventor of the Sykes-Fairbairn knife, who learned his deadly skills in 30 years on the Shanghai waterfront. Fully illustrated.
9781847348531

ART OF BOXING AND SCIENCE OF SELF DEFENCE
Former Lightweight Champion Billy Edwards shares the techniques and strategies of the sweet science in his beautifully illustrated boxing guide. Explore boxing's transition from bare knuckle spectacle to today's Marquis of Queensbury ruleset.
9781474539548

SELF DEFENCE OR THE ART OF BOXING
Ned Donnelly was a pioneer of boxing training during the late Victorian era. Explore the strategies and techniques used by this trainer of champions via a series of easy-to-follow illustrations and clear, concise coaching steps.
9781474539562

JACK GOODWIN'S BOXING

This 1920's boxing masterpiece by Jack Goodwin puts you in the shoes of a coach in that era. Uncover the best ways to run, manage and train boxers as taught by Jack Goodwin, a champion and trainer of champions in the noble science.

9781474539586

ART OF WRESTLING

George de Relwyskow Army Gymnastic Staff

In the appreciation to this book Captain Daniels, V.C., M.C., Rifle Brigade, states: "In adding a word to this book on the style of wrestling as taught at the Headquarters Gymnasium of the British Army, and having had personal experience in the various holds and throws taught, I consider it has been of great value in the training of the soldier, and the bringing out of those qualities of grit and determination which have been seen in all ranks who have taken an active part throughout the greatest war in history." 1919.

9781783313563

THE COMPLETE BOXER

Gunner Moir provides detailed instructions on the techniques he deployed to become British Heavyweight Champion. Taught in a series of easy to learn techniques, combinations, and boxing strategies.

9781474539609

KILL OR GET KILLED

Rex Applegate's "kill or be killed" helped prepare America's marines, soldiers, sailors, spies and airmen for the realities of war. This highly shared and respected work provides all you need to know about unarmed combat and close quarter engagement with the enemy.

9781474539661

BOXING (V-Five)

The Aviation Training Office of the Chief of Naval Operations

The game-changing V-Five suite of training manuals helped get a generation of American aviators fit for war. Here we explore how the airmen of the US navy trained in boxing as part of their military fitness regime.

9781474539623

THE TEXTBOOK OF WRESTLING

Get your wrestling skills matt-ready from wrestling champion and world-renown trainer Ernest Gruhn. Replete with detailed holds, throws, pins and strategies for success in a wide range of wrestling rulesets.

9781474539647

MANUAL OF PHYSICAL TRAINING 1914
(United States Army)

Published just prior to the outbreak of World War 1, this beautifully illustrated guide was designed to revolutionise the combat fitness and readiness of the US Army covering a wide range of gymnastic and combat calisthenic exercises.

9781474539708

DEAL THE FIRST DEADLY BLOW
United States Department of the Army

This Vietnam-era classic showcases in detail how the US Forces trained in close quarter combat. Known as the "encyclopaedia of combat" it helped a generation learn how to become devastating effective with empty hands, knives and bayonets alike.

9781474539722

HAND-TO-HAND COMBAT
Bureau of Aeronautics U.S Navy 1943

This is one of the best combative manuals from World War 2, developed by the US Navy V-Five Staff, that included the renowned American wrestler Wesley Brown. It is then not especially surprising that wrestling skills predominate in this manual, and form the base skill-set for this combative system.

9781474537391

ABWEHR ENGLISCHER GANGSTER METHODEN DEFENSE OF ENGLISH GANGSTERS METHODS – SILENT KILLING – FULL ENGLISH TRANSLATION

In 1942 the Wehrmacht published a training manual with the goal of countering the "silent killing" tactics used by the British commando units. The manual was – much in line with typical National Socialist terminology –titled "Abwehr Englischer Gangster-methoden" or "Defence Against English Gangster methods".

This book was compiled due the Wehrmacht intelligence operatives uncovering of a British hand-to-hand course for the SOE, Commandos, et al, on methods of quick and silent killing (undoubtedly developed by W. E. Fairbairn and E. A. Sykes). They correctly assessed that their troops in general and particularly the Geheime Staatspolizei (Gestapo), Sicherheitsdienst (SD), their security guards, and sentries would be in grave danger when confronted by men trained in these methods. This manual/program was the Wehrmacht's response.

9781474538336

HAND TO HAND COMBAT

Francois d'Eliscu taught thousands of U.S. Army Rangers how to fight down and dirty in World War II.d'Eliscu doesn't get the press that Fairbairn and Applegate do, but he did a commendable job writing this book.It is basic, meant for training raw recruits in a short amount of time before sending them to the front, but simple is good when you are in combat, as most combative experts' will tell you.

9781474535823

WE Fairbairn's Complete Compendium of Lethal, Unarmed, Hand-to-Hand Combat Methods and Fighting In Colour

All 844 images of Fairbairn and his assistants can now for the first time be seen in full colour, lending a clarity to the practical methods of mastering the manner of dealing with an assailant, both in time of war and when placed in difficulty during unpleasant modern urban situations. These various holds, trips, kicks, blows etc. allow the average man or woman a position of security against almost any form of armed or unarmed attack.

Captain W.E. Fairbairn would have approved of this new colour version, that gives an illustrative clarity to the original that was lacking in previous monochrome reprints of his work.

All six of W.E. Fairbairn's works in one binding to create the ultimate colour compendium: Get Tough-All-In Fighting-Shooting to Live-Scientific Self-Defence-Hands Off!-Defend

9781783318735

BOXING FOR BOYS
Regtl. Sergt.-Major E B Dent Army Gymnastic Headquarters

A successful system of boxing instruction for large classes, to allow tuition with no detriment to the "backward or shy pupil". Covers Kit-On, Guard-Sparring-Advance-Point & Mark-Ducking-Medicine, Bag-Left & Right Hooks etc. The author considered that boxing systematically taught to the youth was beneficial exercise, and would have a marked elevating influence on the national character.

9781783314607

HAND-TO-HAND FIGHTING
A System Of Personal Defence For The Soldier (1918)

A tough book on the art of hand to hand fighting in the trenches of the Great War. Demonstrating techniques utilised to "do away with the enemy", many of which are barred in clean wrestling, the book includes good clear photographic illustrations presenting important attack methods including the "Hammer Lock", "Kidney Kick", "Head Twist", "Knee Groin Kick", and the "Knee Break", all very important in a man to man, life or death encounter, when fighting in the mud of the trenches.

9781783313983

COLD STEEL

A cold-war combatives classic. John Styers, US Marine and WW2 veteran, lays out his approach to close quarters combat with rifle, bayonet, stick, knife and empty hands. Explore what helped wartime and post-war Marines stay ahead of the competition with lucid imagery and clear combative descriptions.

9781474540643

THE COMPLETE KANO JIU-JITSU

Join world-famous physical culture expert H. Irving Hancock, and Jiu-Jitsu specialist Katsukama Higashi as they showcase the art of 'Kano Jiu-Jitsu' now known as Judo. Get an exclusive glimpse into the transitional era of the martial art, alongside how it uses Japanese physical culture methodologies for self-improvement.

9781474540735

SCIENTIFIC UNARMED COMBAT

The Art of Dynamic Self-Defence

Learn the esoteric Sri Lankan art of 'Cheena-Adi' with R. A Vairamuttu. This guide explores armed and unarmed self-defence drawing heavily from Indian martial culture, alongside wellness and development from Indian physical culture, fitness, diet and medicine.

9781474540728

SELF DEFENCE FOR WOMEN
COMBATO

Join the Canadian combatives legend William "Bill" Underwood as he showcases self-defence for women. Over the course of clear photography, sketches and instructions he lays out a curriculum for self-defence for the attacks women would be most likely to face.

9781474540711

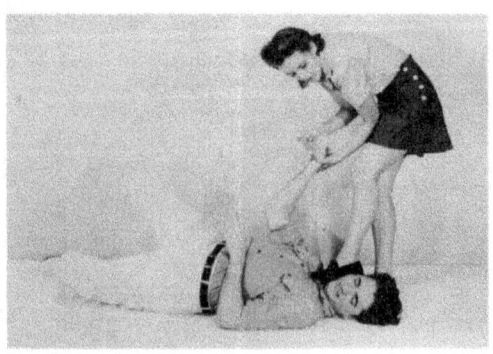

THE NEW SCIENCE
Weaponless Defence

Join wrestling champions Prof F. S Lewis, William V Gregory and Boxing Champ Tommy Burns as they showcase street orientated self-defence from people with a proven track record of fighting success. This 1906 manual via a series of photos and instructions lays out simple, tried and tested ways to keep yourself safe.

9781474540704

COMBAT CONDITIONING MANUAL
Jiu-Jitsu Defence, Bayonet Defence and Club Defence

This 1942 guide for marines lays out the basics of combat Ju Jitsu as part of an overall training regimen for US Marines. It's a holistic guide that covers defences against armed and unarmed attackers, physical fitness and even first aid.

9781474540698

BOXING TAUGHT THROUGH "SLOW MOTION FILM"

Learn the ropes from the best fighters of the 1900s-1930s in this unique boxing manual. Using stills from super slow-mo fight footage, this treasure trove unpacks the skills, tips and tactics of the champs for you to emulate at home.

9781474540681

HOW TO BOX CORRECTLY

Explore the art of boxing according to famous Bronx boxing brand Ben Lee in this 1944 how-to guide. Learn the ropes from one of the nation's top trainers and boxing journalists John J. Romano, in this warmly illustrated guide to the sweet science.

9781474540674

www.ingramcontent.com/pod-product-compliance
Lightning Source LLC
Chambersburg PA
CBHW070305100426
42743CB00011B/2360